The Music of the Future

Robert Barry

Published by Repeater Books
An imprint of Watkins Media Ltd

Unit 11, Shepperton House
89-93 Shpperton Road
London
N1 3DF
UK
www.repeaterbooks.com
A Repeater Books paperback original 2017
3

Distributed in the United States by Random House, Inc.,
New York.

Cover design: Johnny Bull
Typography and typesetting: Josse Pickard
Typefaces: Scala/Scala Sans

ISBN: 978-1-910924-96-9
Ebook ISBN: 978-1-910924-87-7

Printed and bound in the UK by TJ Books Ltd.

for Thanh Mai

Contents

Prelude: 2016

It's about a quarter to eleven on the third of May and I'm at a bar in Zagreb's Studentski Centar. Built in the mid-Thirties for the city's international economic exhibition, since 1957 the complex has acted as a cultural hub for the University of Zagreb. Eighty years ago, the atrium in which I'm standing, along with the &TD Theatre by its side, were part of the trade fair's Italian Pavilion, designed in jutting modernist concrete blocks by the Florentine architect Dante Petroni. Today, it is playing host to another kind of festival: Izlog Suvremenog Zvuka, the 'Showroom of Contemporary Sound', a week-long programme of concerts, talks, and art installations bringing together cutting-edge composers and improvisers from throughout the world.

Over the next few days, I will see and hear artists determinedly pushing at the limits of music from all directions, scoring flickering choreographies of light bulbs, dancing oblique high-wire semaphores with the buzz and fizzing of tasers, collaging the quotidian noises of the city into a propulsive soundscape made magical by the transformative powers of digital manipulation. But right now, we are in a gap between gigs. I'm sipping from a bottle of beer and talking to a local computer programmer and PhD candidate called Antonio Pošćić. Inspired by the concert that just finished, we've got into a deep conversation about writing, music, and code. He's here to review the festival for a blog about free jazz; I'm here because earlier this afternoon I gave an hour-long, rather rambling, and only occasionally coherent lecture entitled 'The Music of the Future'.

In my lecture at the Academy of Music across town, I had tried to trace a line from an article published in 1852 that fingered Robert Schumann, Hector Berlioz, Franz Liszt, and Richard Wagner as "literary musicians," occupied equally with writing critical texts *about* music as they were with writing music itself, to contemporary composers like Holly Herndon and Jennifer Walshe, who are engaging the transformative potential of the internet through the music they write and the statements they make about that music. I wanted to plot the points of a kind of speculative continuum, in which reflection about music, in and through the most important media of the day (from mass publishing to the world wide web), was wielded as a tool to reshape musical practice and carve out a path towards the future of the art form.

But having made the possibly ill-advised decision to talk from memory, without a script or even so much as a hastily scribbled note, and a little nervous about speaking in an academic context quite apart from my usual habitat of pop-culture websites and glossy magazines, I had ended up veering about a little chaotically from one idea to the next, descending into long tangents and looping back to key points I had neglected to cover earlier in the speech. Afterwards, people told me it had been "interesting," if not always totally understandable.

I was even less prepared for the questions that followed. Not so much those from the audience at the lecture itself. They were fine. Smart, interesting, challenging, engaged, and few in number. All good. What caught me off guard was the – on reflection, probably inevitable – line of questioning from people who hadn't come to the talk itself but had simply taken its title at face value.

I soon found myself in the middle of an interview with the Croatian national broadcaster, a mic thrust at my face. The disarmingly cordial interviewer smiled asking, "What will be the future of music?"

"I'm not a fortune-teller," I started to protest. "What I'm interested in, really, is the way composers in the past have used the *idea* of the future to effect changes in the way people think about music that we can still feel today." And already I can sense a certain look stealing onto the face of my interrogator. It's a look that, as a journalist myself, I recognise well. It says: how am I supposed to make a bloody headline out of *that*?

But talking to Antonio in the bar on the night of the lecture, full of the confidence of that second (or was it third?) bottle of Ožujsko, it suddenly occurs to me how to express the point I was trying to get across in my presentation earlier in the day. I cut my new friend off mid-sentence, rather rudely, and start yabbering at him like a cattle auctioneer on a first date.

"I think what I was driving at, earlier," I start to say, "is some idea of a music that would be sufficiently self-conscious to work as criticism – and, by extension, I suppose, a kind of criticism that could at least aspire to some of the qualities of music."

Antonio's brow furrows slightly at this. I plough on regardless. "The important thing about composers like Wagner and Liszt is not just the music they made, but all the various fictions circulating around that. That stuff isn't *getting in the way of* a proper understanding of some supposedly real or authentic

Wagner – it's actively producing all sorts of interesting directions of its own. We need people – whether critics or composers or other artists – to make these kind of stories and confabulations up, to make mistakes and get things wrong. People *should* be abusing each other's work, jamming it up against things it wasn't supposed to go anywhere near – just as we'd expect artists to use technology in ways it wasn't intended for, against the grain of its manufacturer's intentions – because often that's where new ideas and new directions come from, from failure and misuse, and general misapprehension."

The next day Antonio emails me a quote from Tom Arthur's thesis, *The Secret Gardeners: An Ethnography of Improvised Music in Berlin (2012–13)*: "Despite a small selection of dedicated online blogs and specialist publications," Arthur writes, "criticism was on an extremely small scale, and many musicians lamented 'the abysmal quality of journalism' ... few musicians looked to critics for input into their work, with very few following the press on a regular basis, and most taking the opinions of their colleagues more seriously."

"Well," I write back, a little tongue-in-cheek, "we can't expect every critic to be a great artist ... Then again, maybe the musicians were wrong – they resented the local journalists for misinterpreting their work. But in the end, maybe the fiction is more important than the reality."

There is a short story by Ray Bradbury called 'The Toynbee Convector'. First published in *Playboy* magazine in January 1984, it describes the visit of an eager young journalist to interview an old man, known as the Time Traveller. A century before, this Time Traveller had apparently returned from the future – from, in fact, the story's own present day. He had seen the future, he claimed, and it was bright. He even brought with him samples, "tapes and LP records, films and sound cassettes" as proof of the golden tomorrow he had glimpsed from a machine of his own invention.

Inspired by his evidence, the people of the world had built the very future he promised. They had "rebuilt the cities, freshened the small towns, cleaned the lakes and rivers, washed the air, saved the dolphins, increased the whales, stopped the wars, tossed solar stations across space to light the world, colonized the moon, moved on to Mars, then Alpha Centauri."

The day of the young journalist's visit is the anniversary of that auspicious journey to tomorrow, the very day he was said to have transported himself into, a century ago. As a crowd gathers outside to await the appearance in the sky of the Time Traveller's younger self, he finally admits the truth: "I lied."

"Yes," Antonio says to me when I mention Bradbury's story. "I get your point. It's important to believe and continue talking about these ideas. Otherwise we might get stuck in a loop of negative feedback, a self-fulfilling prophecy of sorts. That is to say, a utopian vision of music criticism needs to exist before it can begin shaping music."

I often wonder how Bradbury imagined his Time Traveller filling up those "tapes and LP records" supposed to be from a hundred years time. What materials could he have used, gathered from his own past and present, and collaged together into something resembling the future? Pictures, films even, you can understand how he could have faked. Bradbury had been to Hollywood. As a teenager, attending Los Angeles High School in the mid-Thirties, he used to rollerskate around Melrose Avenue, Figueroa, and North La Brea, in the vicinity of the studio lots, hoping to catch a glimpse of a star.

At the time he wrote 'The Toynbee Convector' he was still two decades from getting his own star on the pavement of the Hollywood Boulevard, but Bradbury had seen half a dozen of his stories get turned into films, and many more become TV – he even adapted *Moby Dick* for John Huston. Suffice to say, he knew plenty about special effects, about how cinema was nothing but lies, twenty-four frames a second. But how could an LP lie?

Sitting at his writing desk in the Cheviot Hills in the early Eighties, feeling, perhaps, a little like his Time Traveller, that "everywhere was professional despair, intellectual ennui, political cynicism," what had Bradbury heard that made him think someone could fake the sounds of the future?

Despite my protestations during that interview in Zagreb, music has a long and deep connection to the crystal ball. In his book *Noise: The Political Economy of Music*, Jacques Attali contends that, from earliest times, music participated intimately in forms of ritual, acting as a herald, the promise of the possibility of a new society to come. For the anthropologist Claude Lévi-Strauss, music is itself a form of myth, albeit encoded differently from language. In the Western Christian tradition, the predominant form of myth-making has been concerned with the past. It spoke of the origin of things, and legitimised the enduring power of the priesthood and the nobility.

In Italian operas of the seventeenth and eighteenth centuries, this kind of mythic legitimation is set to music: works written at the behest of the sovereign would inevitably clothe the figure of the monarch in ancient dress, representing him onstage in the semblance of some semi-divine being or classical hero. But during carnival festivities, the order of social power could be inverted. The music of carnival gave life to the suspension of all the usual hierarchies. This is why works like Josef Haydn's *Il mondo della luna* or Mozart's *Marriage of Figaro*, whose stories derive from the carnival tradition of the Commedia dell'Arte, directly dramatise this upending of social norms. The triumph of servants over their masters, youth over age.

The members of the Florentine Camerata, who developed the first operas at the end of the sixteenth century, were also amongst the first authors of musical manifestos to explicitly invoke the modern. But Giulio Caccini's *Le nuove musiche* and Vincenzo Galilei's *Dialogo della musica antica et della moderna* still somehow managed to cast their innovations as reconstructions of ancient Greek practice. They had no examples at hand to base their "reconstructions" on. None had survived the centuries. In the absence of any antique model, the Camerata confabulated their own history, and secretly made the first truly modern art, unburdened by any real historical precedent. They built myths about their own music.

In the *intermedi* the Camerata wrote and performed for the wedding of Fernando de' Medici and Christina of Lorraine, mythology is staged as a series of dramatic tableaux depicting the 'Harmony of the Spheres', 'Apollo's Battles against Python', the 'Realm of the Spirits', the 'Rescue of Arion', and so forth. Across six short pantomimes, with orchestral accompaniment, elaborate stage effects and machinery, dance numbers, chorus, and solo arias, Caccini, Galilei, and their colleagues cleared a path for the first operas of a decade later, staging myth through music and music as myth. It may be that Vincenzo's son, Galileo Galilei, the man probably responsible more than any other for the broad brushstrokes of our own picture of the cosmos, learned to conceive of the universe as an organic totality whilst playing the lute at these *intermedi* as a young man. His first view of the galaxy was from the orchestra pit.

Around the time of the French Revolution, a strange reversal starts to take place. Though the architects of the guillotine spared no occasion to rhetorically clothe themselves in the outfits of ancient Greece or Rome, the substance of their emotional appeal to the French people dealt not with the past but with the future. Hence, Robespierre, on the eve of the reign of terror in 1793: "The time has come to call upon each to realize his own destiny. The progress of human Reason laid the basis for this great Revolution, and you shall now assume the particular duty of hastening its pace." In the words of the historian Reinhart Koselleck, "For Robespierre, the acceleration of time is a human task, presaging an epoch of freedom and happiness, the golden future."

Few citizens of Robespierre's France conjured the image of that golden future as vividly as Charles Fourier. His writing, by turns lucidly critical and utterly surreal, provides a direct access to the mythic subconscious of Europe on the cusp of modernity.

Fourier grasped eagerly at Robespierre's promise of self-determination. Over the course of the 1790s, he wrote hundreds of letters to various departments of the new government, suggesting improvements to this or that public amenity. Finding his efforts routinely spurned, he eventually gave up on adapting the world he was given and decided to make one up of his own. The *phalanstère* of Fourier's imagining, elaborated over a series of visionary texts and tracts between 1808 and his death in 1837, was like tomorrow's Eden: an earthly paradise, at once both the distantly projected eighth stage of a mammoth thirty-two phase, eighty-thousand-year future history, and, somewhat confusingly, always just around the corner – already, in fact, long overdue. Reading Fourier can be rather like reading philosophy in another dimension, tumbling across the political tract of some fictional character from an imaginary world. Like much good science fiction, one is surprised, having followed for a time a seemingly straightforward scientistic discourse, to suddenly find oneself launched off a precipice, onto an unknown planet, faced with anti-crocodiles and lemonade seas, deep into a discussion of the erotic life of the solar system. But what gradually becomes clear is that his whole project is structured by music.

The key thing for Fourier was never to rely on people's "better natures," but to cater for human passions in all their singular messiness. In the Fourierist phalanstery, there was a place for every perversion, an ideal task suited to each taste, such that every citizen could take pleasure from work that also contributed to the health of the community. This took a phenomenal effort of organisation. But he knew such coordination was possible because he had seen it night after night in the orchestra pit of the theatre. The passions, he believed, could be harmonised, just like a musical scale.

Fourier loved the opera and went whenever he could. With his oft-repeated encomiums to "knight errantry" and amorous intrigues, one is apt to suspect that his idea of utopian life is drawn straight from a libretto, complete with trios, choirs, and soloists, labouring in fine costumes, and all perfectly choreographed as a never-ending corps de ballet. In the disciplined togetherness of dancers and orchestral musicians, he saw the means by which the growing child could "learn to subordinate their movements to the unitary proprieties." Hence the opera, in Fourier's new world, was to be more than mere entertainment, but a "material school", an institution in which all the faculties would be developed equally through active participation in the "material culture" of the community. To the daily life of the phalanstery, the opera house was "as necessary," Fourier maintained, "as its ploughs and herds."

But Fourier's prescriptions went unheeded. By the 1830s, small children had taken to pointing at him in the streets, shouting "Voila! Le fou!" Having declared that the melting of the polar icecaps would soon release a purifying fluid into the world's oceans and turn the water into "a sort of lemonade," his public reputation was at a low ebb. He did have his followers, both in France and abroad. In the years after his death, several attempts at Fourierist phalansteries were established in America – at Utopia, Ohio; La Reunion, Texas; Red Bank, New Jersey; and Brook Farm in Massachusetts. None lasted more than a few years. And every one of them neglected what for Fourier had been the crucial thing: the new world's musical underpinnings.

Keen to distance themselves from the more eccentric side of their Master, the American Fourierists emphasised his critique of capitalism and his social egalitarianism over the lemonade seas and musical games, the complex divisions of his octave of passions. Only many years later did the Surrealists, André Breton and Georges Bataille, realise that these two sides of Fourier were inseparable. "If it is possible to regret it has not engendered more positive results," wrote Bataille of Fourier's system, "how can one not recognise that poetry alone could be their initiation?"

Fourier's poetry may have fallen on deaf ears, but we can still hear its traces, rippling through the musical history of the nineteenth century and beyond. In Berlioz's futuristic fantasy of a musical city called Euphonia, whose every waking moment was spent in preparation for its annual opera festival. In the very real opera festival created by Wagner at Bayreuth, which transformed the small Bavarian town into a secular temple, dedicated to music. On every occasion when large numbers of people gather, in a place not quite city and not quite countryside, to set aside the usual rules governing social discourse, and organise their coming together around music instead. Whether consciously or not, such moments have just a touch of the phalanstery about them – even if the lemonade seas have all too often become rivers of slurry and cold lager. So, with all that in mind, the next time I was interviewed in Zagreb, and asked about the music of the future, I found myself a little better prepared.

"Festivals like this one," I said this time, "could be building the foundations for the future of music. Events like this, not governed by the commercial imperatives of record labels and talent agencies, nor by the territorial policing of academic departments – offer up a space for musicians to come together in a kind of free association, to present their work and ideas and make surprising connections across disciplines. In a way, what's important here is not any of the individual performances, but the conversations that take place amongst artists between the shows, the fictions and fissures that open up in the gaps between styles and approaches. There's a model, there, perhaps, for some kind of community, a promise that society is possible."

Over the pages that follow, I won't be presuming, like Ray Bradbury's Time Traveller, to provide a map for the way music should develop and transform itself over the next century. What I want to present is something more like a history of failures – failures to meet the impossible challenge of the music of the future, to summon up a whole world in a verse or a song. But this succession of failures nonetheless left their marks on the way we continue to think and feel about music. They opened up spaces of possibility, through reflection, dialogue, new work and ideas. And with that, maybe there's a covert challenge, following Samuel Beckett, to "Try again. Fail again. Fail better."

First Act: 1913

On the first of November 2010, I was at Cafe Oto in London for an event billed as 'An Audience with Terry Riley'. Over the course of a long onstage chat, the composer of *In C* and *A Rainbow in Curved Air* answered questions about his early work with magnetic tape, his friendships with musicians like La Monte Young and Pandit Pran Nath – even his favourite colour.

Towards the end of the event, I finally plucked up my courage and asked the question that had been on my mind throughout. "You've been called a 'visionary' composer before," I began, umming and ahhing uncertainly. "So how do you imagine the music of the future?"

My question was greeted with a ripple of what I took at the time to be somewhat derisory laughter, both from the stage and from the audience. "You're trying to put me on the spot!" chuckled Riley uncomfortably. I pictured him signalling covertly to the security guards.

He didn't, of course. Anyone who has ever been in the same room as Terry Riley will, I suspect, recognise him as a very warm-spirited man. He's the sort of person you'd like to have around at Christmas. You can imagine him turning up at the end of a film to pat the hero on the back and thank god everything's back to normal again. "All I can say is," he finally replied, "that I just hope there *is* a future." The compere, swiftly, shepherded the conversation onto other matters.

And who can blame him? How can anyone even begin to answer a question like that? I was embarrassed just asking it. But at the same time I was worried.

At the beginning of the twenty-first century there seemed to be a lot of talk about the future of music. Every few months a new book or article would come out with that title, or some slight variation on it. For the most part they were not being written by musicians. At least, that's how it seemed to me. As if the future of music was not being set out by music people at all, but by tech sort of people: dot-com entrepreneurs, digital-marketing gurus, social-media ninjas, and other habitués of the TED-talk circuit. Even when musicians did chime in, the terms of the debate were so dominated by the noise from Silicon Valley that they seemed to be left little choice but to either nod along in agreement or come across like some sort of crazed luddite, choked with nostalgia, trying to bring back the horse-drawn victrola.

I kept trying to find someone who could provide an alternative perspective, someone who might just have ideas more imaginative than how best to monetise file torrenting or build a sustainable YouTube empire. Musicians themselves struck me as a good bet.

After all, music has a long, native futurist tradition. Long before American military engineers had dreamed of a man-machine symbiosis, Hector Berlioz had pictured the orchestra as a cybernetic organism and a living, breathing factory. Long before the hippie back-to-the-landers conspired with the world of corporate R&D to re-fashion the computer as a tool for global communion, Richard Wagner had looked forward to the united artistic community of the future and presented opera as a means of changing society sufficiently to bring such a thing about. Opera had long been music's privileged conduit to the future, from the Wagnerian *Gesamtkunstwerk* to the Russian Futurists. It promised a world on a stage, a time beyond the clock.

So undaunted, a little over five years later, I found an opportunity to try again.

I was spending the weekend at a music festival called Borealis in the Norwegian city of Bergen. Arriving on a Thursday afternoon, I spent most of the day getting lost amongst the city's maze-like cobbled streets. I remember, in particular, getting so lost and battered by the North Sea winds, trying to find a venue along the waterfront to the north of the city centre, that I finally gave up, only then to stumble upon the very place, just as I was turning round to give up. I had to creep in at the back of the hall in the middle of a whisper-quiet performance by the local sinfonietta. Later that evening, thankfully, I managed to get a lift to the Cornerteatret across town, where the American group Object Collection would be premiering their new opera, *It's All True*.

Arriving at the theatre, a little early, I soon realised there was nowhere nearby to get anything to eat. Having spent the day staggering around with no idea where I was going, desperately trying not to miss whatever was next on the programme, I was, by this point, starving. My options were limited. I bought a cup of peanuts and a cup of olives from the bar and sat down, greedily shovelling from both pots into my mouth until the bell rang for the start of the performance. I took my seat with a tongue like a big, floppy salt-and-vinegar crisp, quite ill-prepared for what was about to happen.

It's All True proved to be quite unlike the usual fare at Covent Garden. The work's authors, Kara Feely and Travis Just, had begun their process of composition by sitting through some thousand hours of amateur footage of the American post-hardcore band Fugazi, shot between 1986 and 2002. Meticulously, they scored and scripted every word spoken, sung, or shouted, every note of music played or incidentally struck – except, that is, for the band's actual songs. What results, written out for a group of four electric guitarists, two drummers, and a quartet of actor-singers, is a disjointed collage of accumulated out-takes, an epic tragicomedy about a band that took themselves far too seriously, a raucous assault on the politics of America in the Clinton-Bush years – not to mention on the ears of the audience. It is a relentless work, a cacophony of simultaneous actions maintaining the same fevered pitch throughout its almost two-hour length. The crowd, upon leaving, looked positively shell-shocked. Was I ill? I wasn't sure.

Over the days that followed, it became clear the work had sharply divided its audience. Many were thrilled by it, others baffled, or even irritated. I heard several people complain that it went on too long or that it lacked the proper differentiation between parts. But it was clearly the thing that everyone was talking about. People who had been almost angered by the work upon leaving the theatre would find themselves still going on about it three days later, and would then start to question their own response. Only later did I realise how faithful *It's All True* had been to the aesthetic ideas of Richard Foreman, as laid down in his 'Ontological-Hysteric' manifestos of the early Seventies.

Foreman, who both Feely and Just have assisted in productions in New York, had wanted to "destroy" the stage "carefully, not with effort," as he put it, "but with delicate manoeuvres." He graduated from Brown at the end of the Fifties, having set up the university theatre group, The Production Workshop. Returning to his home town of New York, he fell in with experimental composers and filmmakers like La Monte Young and Jack Smith who were then in the process of upsetting all sorts of apple carts in their own respective art forms.

By 1967, Foreman began to feel like the theatre as it was seemed "ridiculous in all its manifestations." He wanted to bring a sense of danger back onto the stage, to confront his audiences with a "perpetual motion machine" of simultaneous yet contradictory actions. "The artistic experience," he wrote in 1971, "must be an ordeal to be undergone." Yes, I thought when I read that, that's what *It's All True* was like.

On the Friday morning of the festival, the Bergen Kunsthall hosted a discussion on 'Opera's Bold Future'. Just and Feely were joined on the panel by other festival participants, Lore Lixenberg, Jennifer Walshe, and Lars Petter Hagen, to discuss "what the future holds for opera." But for the most part the speakers seemed more concerned with opera's past, wringing their hands over the "baggage" that accompanies the term, and swapping strategies for escaping it.

"The history of opera," Lixenberg said, "is in some ways a curse." A celebrated mezzo soprano herself, Lixenberg admitted it can be "a barrier" when you bring up opera to someone in the street. "But in fact opera is still an amazingly relevant, fabulous thing," she continued. "Using last night's Object Collection performance as a reference point, what was so exciting was that it was this perfect melting together of image, music, and text to create something which is greater than the sum of its parts."

After about three-quarters of an hour, they opened up to questions from the floor. I grabbed my chance. Alluding to the title of the panel, I asked, "Why do we so often find these two words – 'opera' and the 'future' – placed together? What is the connection here, between opera and the future?"

No laughter this time. Just silence. For a moment I could almost see the tumbleweed rolling across what started to feel like an aching chasm between the seated figures with microphones over there and me, cross-legged on the floor and sweaty, in the audience. Finally, Travis Just responded, albeit somewhat briefly.

About a year earlier, Just had written an essay called 'After Opera' for the collection *Arcana VII: Musicians on Music*, edited by the American composer John Zorn. In this essay, Just argued for a profound reassessment of the genre. Every element of the standard definition of opera – the music, the text, the drama – all had by now been so thoroughly overhauled, he claimed, that the standard definition was next to useless. Better to seek what he called an "anti-synthesis" of quasi-autonomous components circulating around an absent centre. Opera, he argued, was a paradoxical, perfectly "incomplete artwork," and all the more abundant with possibilities because of it. But when I asked about opera's tie to the future, he said, "I'd love to go backwards in time – but it's not an option."

More silence.

After the talk I was standing outside the Kunsthall smoking a rolled-up cigarette. Mary Miller, the head of the local opera company in Bergen, walked out of the main doors. I had noticed her seated by the side of the room in the talk just previously. She gave me a slightly quizzical look as she passed me but carried on walking just the same. Then, a few steps further on, she stopped and spun around. Walking back to where I stood, she wore the expression of someone chewing over a thought. "That is an interesting question," she said to me. "I mean, no one ever asks about the future of literature..."

She's right. The talk we had attended came on the heels of a whole slew of articles in the press about the future of opera, very few of them optimistic. New York City Opera had filed for bankruptcy in 2013. Half the houses in Italy were said to be essentially broke. London's English National Opera was scarcely faring any better. "Who can we trust with the future of opera?" *The Telegraph* had asked on the first of September 2015. At the Battle of Ideas Festival at the Barbican Centre a month later, a panel asked, 'A Dying Art? The Future of Opera'.

In many other articles from the period, everyone from critics to administrators to world-famous tenors are quoted worrying about "opera's perilous future." Lurking somewhere around most of these debates were all the old prejudices: that opera is old-fashioned, elitist, stuffy, unnatural, a waste of funds, cosseted and indulgent, hopelessly irrelevant to young people and out of touch with the modern world. All of these things had been said for three hundred years and they had all just been proved wrong by last night's performance of *It's All True*.

1.2 Tropical Fish Opera

Reading through some of the hand-wringing about the state of opera in the press over recent years, one is apt to get the impression that the genre is a closed world of bizarre old rituals, abstrusely encoded in order explicitly to alienate Lore Lixenberg's notional man in the street. Nothing could be further from the truth.

"The term is super-open right now," Lars Petter Hagen had said, somewhere near the beginning of that panel talk in Bergen. Hagen has himself composed several fascinating operatic works, including a "documentary opera" realised with the artist duo Goksøyr & Martens, co-written and performed by pupils at Barnato Park High School in Johannesburg, based on material from their own dreams. Since 2009, he has also been artistic director to Norway's biggest contemporary music festival, Ultima.

In the autumn of 2015 I was fortunate enough to be able to attend Ultima's twenty-fifth anniversary edition in Oslo. It was inspiring to see such resources mobilised behind new music. A collaboration between groups from the national arts council to the city government to the Norwegian composers' society, Ultima brought artists from all over the world together with the very best ensembles in the country, to produce new, experimental works in places like the city's main concert hall, several of its best theatres, and even the national opera house. But the performance that really stayed with me didn't take place in any of these venues. It happened outside, in the streets.

It started at noon in a carpark with eight young men in black jeans, dark jackets, and white earbuds drumming on a large steel gate. For several minutes they stood there in a line, striking the metal with batons over and again. But in each percussionists' headphones a click track gave them their own unique tempo, so the rhythms phased and undulated like a Steve Reich tape piece.

Soon they shot off, through the gate and up the street, knocking sticks against the pavement, the walls, signposts, whatever, eking out the hidden resonances of the city. They charged up through narrow side roads according to a choreography dictated by a spoken score, synced up through mobile phones directly to their ears. They would all freeze at once, bar maybe one member, left tapping out a pulse on his own for a few bars, before his fellows rejoined him to carry on.

Moving through the city into more and more populated parts of town, all the other noises we could hear started to feel like they were being brought into the concert, given a frame by the ever-changing rhythms, and made musical: the roar of automobile engines, the beep of traffic lights, and the tweet of birds in roadside trees became the bassline, ostinato, and lead vocal to the roving polyrhythmic beat.

Sound Stencil o.1 by Koka Nikoladze finally ended, some forty-five minutes after it began, with all eight drummers pounding together upon some great pylon in the very centre of town. I don't know how it all must have seemed to people going about their Saturday who just caught some brief moment, here or there. But following the journey from start to finish made every surface in the city come alive.

Nikoladze's composition brought together almost all of the elements that we traditionally associate with the opera house: music, dance, an expansive stage setting, even a narrative of sorts, as the group passed from the recently redeveloped Grünerløkka district in the north of the city, through various residential and commercial neighbourhoods, to a central square named after Oslo's once-richest man. Following the definition by the Austrian composer Peter Ablinger, of opera as a meeting point for different modes of "perception and action" potentially encompassing sound installation, instrumental theatre, and interactive music forms, Nikoladze's work here feels central. As Ablinger says of the kind of contemporary opera that most interests him, *Sound Stencil o.1* draws the listener into the work in order to "perceive him/herself perceiving."

Ablinger admits that his notion of opera departs somewhat from the "historical" definition. But he's also aware that that departure itself has copious precedents. La Monte Young's *Poem, a Chamber Opera in One Act* of May 1960 combined spoken texts with bursts of Beethoven, electronic music, people moving and speaking and singing throughout the audience, and several more people apparently preparing a fried breakfast onstage.

At the last Sonics concert organised by Pauline Oliveros and Ramon Sender at San Francisco Conservatory in 1962, a *Smell Opera* was performed in which members of the Ann Halprin Dance Company moved through the audience, spraying people with perfume samples, while playing over the top was a spoken-word religious drama off a reel of tape that one of the composers had found lying in the street. Later the same evening, Sender's *Tropical Fish Opera* brought a large fish tank centre stage to act as a score for music played by Sender, Oliveros, Morton Subotnick, and Loren Rush, but composed by the movements of the fish themselves.

When Laurie Anderson started performing, in late-Seventies New York, she was in a milieu of sculptors, painters, performance artists, comedians, musicians, "and at one point," she told me over the phone in 2010, "we were all working on operas. We called them that. And it was weird," she continued. "You would be walking down the street and go, how's your opera? Mine's fine, how's yours? Everybody was doing it, and we didn't know what it was."

1.3 Every Mark, Blotch, and Stain

To understand the history of opera up to this point, it is instructive to think of three almost consecutive remarks from Sol Le Witt's 'Sentences on Conceptual Art'. "All ideas are art if they are concerned with art and fall within the conventions of art," goes the seventeenth sentence in the American conceptual artist's manifesto of 1969. And then the nineteenth and twentieth statements read, "The conventions of art are altered by works of art," and, "Successful art changes our understanding of the conventions by altering our perceptions."

Like contemporary art, to talk about opera today is not to describe a particular content or settled form, but to grasp at an always-moving point on a dynamic continuum whose evolution stretches back to at least the sixteenth century. Every step on that journey, every great work and every heated debate, has changed the way we understand both the future of the art and its past. Any attempt to pin it down and delineate its features, like some rare species of butterfly stuck to a board, will inevitably be futile, since someone will always come along and say, ah! But what about this...?

In 1956, for instance, the musicologist Joseph Kerman published his *Opera as Drama*, later dubbed by the *New Grove Dictionary of Opera* as "the most influential recent book on opera criticism ... in the English-speaking world." In this book, Kerman seeks explicitly to redefine and reorient opera as "properly a musical form of drama." But in that very same year, Robert Ashley returned from a stint in the army to Ann Arbor, Michigan, where he took up a job at Bell Labs' Speech Research Institute investigating voice synthesis and the causes of stuttering. The following year, he and a friend, Gordon Mumma, took on the role of in-house composers to something called the 'Space Theatre' at the University of Michigan, a state-of-the-art array of projections and coloured lights dancing across the stage to an electronic score. Both of these experiences would provide the foundation stones for the series of operas Ashley began just over five years later with *In Memoriam... Kit Carson*.

Ashley's operas – most famously *Perfect Lives*, a seven-part "TV opera," developed at the Kitchen in New York in the late Seventies and screened by Channel 4 in 1983 – contain a great deal of competing elements, multilayered stories, vivid imagery and interesting music (the latter both, often, electronically generated). What they do not tend to call for is an opera house, elaborate staging, an orchestra pit (or, indeed, an orchestra), bel canto singing, or very much in the way of *drama* – at least as far as drama was understood at the time (Kerman, following T.S. Elliot, had called it "the response of persons in the play to the elements of the action").

Since, as Richard Foreman was realising around the same time, the model of drama that existed then was starting to look increasingly hokey, Ashley preferred to "Let people do what they normally would do, only with an audience present." His works are now recognised as one of the most significant contributions to operatic form in the last hundred years, with *Fanfare* magazine calling his *Perfect Lives* "nothing less than the first American opera." The Irish composer Jennifer Walshe, speaking on that panel at the Borealis Festival in Bergen, called Ashley "one of the best opera composers – ever."

"It's not like we got up to 1905 and then just skipped a hundred years," Travis Just said on the same panel. "There's a long, rich history of things that are all over the place."

"But if it's just a matter of saying, it's something big, let's call it an opera," a voice from the audience objected, "– why not say it's a 'happening'?"

"Opera can be very small," Just replied, hefting one foot onto the knee of his other leg and teasing at the fastening on his footwear. "I'm doing one right now with my shoelace." He wasn't being deliberately provocative. Nor does the kind of expanded definition he's talking about need to be seen as a sign of decadence, or some kind of anything-goes attitude.

"People are actually doing stuff like that," said Lars Petter Hagen.

"I know!" Just agreed.

Perhaps what separates Travis Just's generation of composers from Laurie Anderson's is precisely that they *do* know *what it is*. Experimental art today is rarely a shot in the dark; more likely, it is a considered engagement with a detailed and often contradictory history. Contemporary composers are very aware of that history. It's kind of difficult not to be. There's so much information now available on the web or in print, so many old recordings being reissued, so much video documentation on YouTube or UbuWeb, that the weight of material available could almost start to seem like a burden in itself, like so much baggage on one's shoulders. Writing his book *Retromania* at the beginning of the twenty-first century's second decade, the music critic Simon Reynolds grew concerned that this overwhelming presence of the past could prove to be "the greatest danger to the future of our music culture."

"The relation to history is now, for a lot of people, more and more important," Lars Petter Hagen said to the panel at Borealis. "The modernist dream of making something completely new – nobody believes in that anymore."

I tend to think that, actually, new things are being made all the time. Even just over the few days I spent in Bergen, I saw the American collective Ensemble Pamplemousse making complex, considered music with computer-controlled slide whistles. I experienced a composition by Danish composer Simon Løffler which required the audience to bite down on a dowel rod in order to hear the music through their teeth. I saw the footwork producer Jlin take electronic dance music into thrilling new worlds of rhythmic complexity and digital psychedelia, a stream of effervescent polyrhythms tumbling from her touch like so many sentient marbles released upon the dancefloor.

But at the same time, in the back of my mind, I could hear the voice of the writer Owen Hatherley, who once said to me, on the subject of recent pop music, "a well-informed observer from 1976, suddenly exposed to the most forward-looking music of 1996, would have encountered something completely alien. A similarly clued-up time-traveller leaping from 1996 to the present day, on the other hand, would probably appreciate several interesting developments, but they would recognise them as just that: more or less predictable extensions to a known field. They wouldn't need to ask, what *is* this?"

I'm not sure if I really buy the idea that the new is being drowned out by dint of our seemingly limitless access to the old. All artists know how inspiring it can be to encounter the work and ideas of other great artists. Many of the artists of the past who, today, we think of as great revolutionaries were incredibly well-informed about their predecessors. Somehow it just doesn't seem to make sense that originality should be precluded by a thorough knowledge of what's gone before. After all, didn't George Santayana say, "Those who cannot remember the past are condemned to repeat it." Shouldn't the same hold for music?

Maybe the problem is not history itself, but the way we have come to relate to it. When I read *Retromania*, I kept thinking of a novel by Walter M. Miller called *A Canticle for Leibowitz*. The book was first published in 1960 and is set six hundred years after some future atomic catastrophe, but it remains just as eloquent about our own culture of reissues, reformations, and gatefold audiophile editions of whatever newly-appointed lost legend's rediscovered demo tapes. It's about an order of monks in a desolate wasteland, patiently copying and illuminating the shopping lists and trivial memoranda of a long-dead electrical engineer onto treated lambskin. Miller's protagonist, Brother Francis, determines to duplicate precisely "every mark, blotch, and stain" on his holy relic (an old engineering blueprint) much as garage-rock revivalists like Billy Childish and Jack White spend their fortunes on valve studio equipment, fetishising antiquated recording equipment and "stripped back" production styles (mono, analogue, live, untreated, etc.). There's a tendency to hark at golden ages, to duplicate to the last detail, but ignore the social conditions that produced those great works in the first place. Somewhere along the way, the meaning gets lost in the scuffle over minutiae. Meanwhile, the future is being written in broad brushstrokes on Canadian conference stages and in

Californian boardrooms.

In order to recover that feeling for the future that today's artists seem wary of speaking about, it may be necessary to peel back the layers of the recent future, the future of intelligent machines and augmented living, of long tails and data sonification, and try to recover some of music's own native futurism. As the present grows stymied and tentative, unsure of its own direction, it might be worth turning to time travel once more, to go back to the music of the future.

1.4 Tele-Theatre

If you had picked up a copy of *Modern Electrics* magazine in April 1911, you would have found guides for 'The Practical Electrician', a description of a 'Condenser for High-Power Transmitters', as well as reports of new inventions from Europe, and various readers' letters (including one from a fifteen year-old Lewis Mumford). Published since 1908, *Modern Electrics* was the first regular magazine to cater explicitly to a burgeoning audience of electrical enthusiasts and radio hams. From very early on, the magazine's editor and publisher Hugo Gernsback deliberately courted his audience as a self-conscious network of hobbyists who were encouraged to communicate their thoughts and activities with the magazine and with each other. The principle means he used to do this was the magazine's letters page.

But in the spring of 1911, Gernsback added something unusual to his editorial content. Tucked in amongst the how-tos and the circuit diagrams was the first instalment of a story he had written himself entitled *Ralph 124C 41+*. Opening in an American home in the year 2660, the story promised to be "as accurate a prophecy of the future as is consistent with the present marvellous growth of science." He called it a work of "scientifiction," but it wouldn't take long for him to ditch that term, in favour of the much less awkward coinage "science fiction." The story's eponymous hero is one of the world's top "super-scientists," one of only ten in the world. Ralph is a man of the future, a model for young inventors everywhere. He speaks to his colleagues via "telephot," writes up his notes by transmitting them directly from his brain by aid of the "menoscope," and when he sleeps his "hypnobioscope" channels chapters from Homer's *Odyssey* straight into his dreams.

In one early scene, Ralph takes a pair of house guests down to his "tele-theatre." It is described as a "large room" with a "shallow stage at one end, with proscenium arch and curtain." A switchboard of cords and plugs connects Ralph's tele-theatre to a performance of an opéra comique called *La Normande*, live from New York. "A great number of loud-speaking telephones were arranged near the stage, and the acoustics were so good," Gernsback writes, "that it was hard to realise that the music originated four miles away at the National Opera House." The tele-theatre is a marvel of twenty-seventh-century technology, capable of broadcasting a perfect representation of the action taking place on a distant stage. Every actor appears full-size and perfectly life-like, their voices carried by telephot as clear as a bell. "Between the acts," the story goes on, "Ralph explained that each New York playhouse now had over 200,000 subscribers and it was as easy for the Berlin and Paris subscribers to hear and see the play as for the New York subscriber."

The thing that strikes me about this passage is the extraordinary lengths Gernsback goes to in order to maintain the nature and form of opera as he knew it. The actors, singers, stage, and scenery have remained perfectly preserved from the nineteenth-century opera house, unaffected by their new means of dissemination – instead, the domestic interior itself has been rearranged to accommodate the presence of a whole little theatre, complete with proscenium arch and curtain.

To some extent this attitude is still alive today. You can see it when you watch most operas that have been filmed for DVD release, or at any of the much-vaunted high-definition broadcasts from the New York Met or London's Royal Opera House. Shot in a style somewhere between rock concert video and daytime television drama, the cinematic language inevitably looks and feels all wrong. Very quickly the jarring close-ups and conspicuous crane shots work to alienate you from the music and the story. Nobody seems to have learnt from Robert Ashley's recognition, some three and a half decades ago, that an opera on television only really works when it's expressly designed as a TV opera. This attitude comes across very clearly in a speculative 2012 piece for *Opera News* by Philip Kennicott. He imagines a future in which "the 'opera house' is now simply a space, anywhere in the world, equipped with the technology to project a fully embodied three-dimensional facsimile of live opera." But still he pictures "Siegmund singing to a holographic Sieglinde."

Kennicott can conceive of a complete transformation in the way opera is presented and experienced with seemingly no thought of any change to the operas themselves. "It could be a warehouse in Topeka," he continues, "or an empty stage in an old movie house that has fallen into disuse." Into that space Kennicott seems to envision the teleportation of *Don Giovanni* apparently oblivious to his changed circumstances, just like in Gernsback's tele-theatre. But for a while back in the twentieth century, there was an idea that the new bottles of the international telecommunications network might benefit from being filled with some new wine.

In May of 1927, an American airmail pilot named Charles Lindbergh shot to fame after flying solo, non-stop, from New York to Paris, in a record thirty-three and a half hours. Rush-released within two months of the expedition, Lindbergh's autobiography, *We*, had carried the suggestion of the flight as not so much a solo mission, more a joint effort; an enterprise shared symbiotically by the man and his flying machine. Bertolt Brecht, then a young playwright in Berlin, was clearly taken by this idea. He was inspired to devise a man-machine interface of his own, a work that would use the technology of the mass media to inspire and empower ordinary people. He determined to compose an opera especially for the radio.

Brecht would not have called it an opera himself. He harboured a suspicion of the term. Too much baggage. In fact, Brecht was pretty suspicious of music in general, preferring what he called "misuc," which would be something like "the singing of working women in a back courtyard on Sunday afternoons," as his friend, the composer Hanns Eisler, would recall. "In misuc nobody may wear tails and nothing may be ceremonious." But the *Lehrstücke* (or "learning plays") that Brecht created around then were, on the whole, dramatic productions with sung dialogue, tending to be heavily reliant on the music of Kurt Weill and Paul Hindemith who, as composers, were involved in the conception of the work from the get-go. They were also received, at least, largely as music: reviewed in the music press, and premiered at major music festivals. *Der Lindberghflug*, Brecht, Weill, and Hindemith's work based on *We*, was first performed at the Donaueschingen Festival (albeit temporarily relocated fifty miles up the road to Baden-Baden), one of the most revered contemporary music festivals going. In style and substance it resembles operas from the period like Arnold Schoenberg's *Von heute auf morgen*, Ernst Krenek's *Jonny spielt auf*, and Hindemith's own *Neues vom Tage*. There is just one major difference between *Der Lindberghflug* and its contemporaries: *Der Lindberghflug* had a hole where its leading man was supposed to be.

The idea was that, when broadcast, the part of Lindbergh himself would be omitted, with scripts distributed in advance for audiences to sing, speak, or hum the part themselves from the comfort of their kitchens. But the scheme rarely went quite as planned. At Baden-Baden, they played it on a split stage, partitioned down the middle, with the orchestra and other parts on one side, dressed in their concert blacks, and on the other side sat Josef Witt, relaxing in his shirtsleeves in a mock-up of a domestic dining room, singing Charles Lindbergh *as if* he hadn't left the house. As it started, Brecht went around the concert hall trying to encourage people to stand outside and listen through the loudspeakers that had been placed on the exterior of the hall, as if determined that the work should not be experienced without some form of technological mediation. For the most part people ignored him.

Despite numerous revisions over subsequent years, *Der Lindberghflug* was never broadcast over the radio *sans* Lindbergh as originally intended. No domestic audience was ever given to sing that part. But in the very year that the real Lindbergh flew across the Atlantic, a recent émigré to the United States called Edgard Varèse was seized by the thought of a radio opera of his own. And the story would be out of this world.

"I'm going to cut loose in my next work," Varèse wrote in a letter to a friend in November 1928, "and give myself the luxury of living in the year 3000." Over the subsequent two decades, the composer's plans would go through many revisions, changing its name (one minute *The One-All-Alone*, the next *L'Astronome*, later *Espace*), changing its librettist (at various times Alejo Carpentier, Robert Desnos, Antonin Artaud, André Malraux), altering its form and its technical means over and over again. What remained relatively consistent was the image of an astronomer in his observatory receiving radio communications from an alien civilisation in a far-off galaxy.

From this germ of an idea, Varèse dreamed up what might have been the very first multimedia opera, in the modern sense of that term. Electronic music could scarcely be said to have even existed in the early Thirties. This did not prevent Varèse practically willing it into existence with a plan to hang loudspeakers throughout his performance space in order to spread electrically-generated sounds through space. Certainly no-one – aside from the likes of Hugo Gernsback – was talking about anything like telematic performance, but Varèse wanted to place singers in the four corners of the world, linked up live by radio transmission, and all singing together in a wireless paleo-cyberspace. There were to be coloured lights, filmed projections, onstage acrobatics, and sounds drawn from sirens and aeroplane propellors. The climax of the piece sounds like total pandemonium: stock markets crashing, fleets of ships disappearing into the sea, angry mobs roaming the stage, and even Charles Lindbergh's plane vanishing from the sky.

But it never happened. Varèse spent decades working on the piece, going through draft after draft of the libretto and enough musical and scenographic ideas to leave the rest of the twentieth century struggling to catch up. Only a few disjointed scraps of score, with one unfinished, rejected draft of a libretto, remain to serve as evidence.

In the end, *The One-All-Alone* or *L'Astronome* or *Espace* seems to have simply become too grandiose to admit any possibility of realisation. Its composer's vision exceeded reality. Bits of it, though, did make their way into other works. Tantalising glimpses, like *hrönir* slipping from another world into ours, would pop up here and there: one fragment became a standalone work, *Ionisation*, the first composition in the Western canon for percussion instruments alone; the "sonic beams," originally intended to be played by ondes martenots, found their way into the *poo-wip* electronic noises of his *Poème électronique* for the Philips Pavilion at the Brussels Expo in 1958; and *Déserts*, his magisterial work for orchestra and tape of the early Fifties, held onto some of the radiophonic element, since Varèse managed to get two different French broadcasters to transmit the first performance at once, so that listeners with two radios at home could tune one into each station and hear it in stereo.

"What interests me about Varèse," Henry Miller wrote in his

Air-Conditioned Nightmare of 1945, "is the fact that he seems unable to get a hearing." Miller's essay collection drew together a series of observations made by the ex-pat author, driving through his homeland upon returning from self-imposed exile in France. At that time, in the 1940s, Varèse was becoming the object of a strange kind of fascination, as if he were not so much an artist as a mad scientist, his brow forever furrowed as he stared intently out of photographs. His music was considered cold and cerebral – there was even a rumour that the scientists behind the Manhattan Project had spent their time working on the Bomb listening to Varèse.

But outside of Oak Ridge and Los Alamos, his music was little performed – and unloved when it was. No composer of the early twentieth century thought so much about the audience, put so much emphasis on the relationship between the work and its listeners, and was yet so spurned by them. At the premiere of his *Hyperprism*, the crowd laughed through the work; during *Déserts*, they sneered openly. "The situation," Miller concluded, "is all the more incomprehensible because his music is definitely the music of the future."

1.5 Etherphone

"On the terrace of one of the sky-palace apartment houses with which our Island of Manhattan will bristle, the New Yorker of the future sits in the twilight and out of the blue ether plucks his own music... Stretch out the hand. Command the ether... A high, thin note, swelling to grandeur, pulsates from the imagination of the man of the future." This is how the pages of *New York American* magazine welcomed to the United States the Russian inventor Lev Sergeyevich Termen in December 1927.

Though it was originally intended to be something so prosaic as a burglar alarm, Termen's invention – which he called an "etherphone," though most people named it "theremin" after its creator – suggested to those who witnessed it a kind of acoustic action-at-a-distance, a technology so fabulous that it resembled sorcery. Hugo Gernsback even ran a cover story in one of his magazines depicting the 'Orchestra of the Future': sixteen theremins on a podium with a conductor in tails waving his hands before them all.

Over the decades Varèse spent beavering away at his *Astronome*, the concerns of music and science fiction never seemed so close. Operas like Karl-Birger Blomdahl's *Aniara* brought space travel to the proscenium stage, in a story about the last surviving earthlings, hurtling through the stars on a ship piloted by computer. Composers like George Antheil and Hans Stuckenschmidt explored "machine music," playing clunky, angular rhythms on gramophones and player pianos in concert settings. The earliest electronic instruments crept out of their inventors' labs to be hailed by the popular press as each heralding the future of music.

Gernsback himself patented two different devices for turning electrical impulses into sound: the Staccatone and the Pianorad, both polyphonic, keyboard-based instruments that used valve-driven oscillators to create and combine pure sine tones. He also published how-to instructions for readers at home to build theremins of their very own – instructions which would catch the attention of a young Robert Moog, some years before he built his first modular synthesizer.

By the 1950s, Termen's invention had become ineluctably linked with alien visitors and flying saucers thanks to its frequent use in science fiction films like *The Day the Earth Stood Still* and *The Thing from Another World*. That quavering, silvery sound, whose swooping glissandi seemed to match the streamline design of the space age, would invariably poke out of the massed strings of the Hollywood studio orchestra whenever a director needed to evoke the inhuman or uncanny, whenever unconvincingly-costumed Martians were approaching. The association was already implied somewhat by Gernsback's 'Orchestra of the Future' cover spread, simply thanks to the style of the illustration, being so similar in its manner of depiction to the space stations and extraterrestrial worlds that usually graced the exteriors of his magazines.

What was missing from such references in the popular press was any sense that music – in its aesthetic values and social relations – would really change. The theremin, and other similar devices (whether Gernsback's own Staccatone or such singular oddities as the Trautonium, the Sphärophon, or the Croix Sonore) were greeted enthusiastically, but rather in the manner of technical novelties, like 3D specs. Brief fads to be marvelled over and quickly forgotten, leaving the way people think about music and sound fundamentally unchanged. The conductor of Gernsback's orchestra of the future still wore tails and commanded autocratically. Concert demonstrations of the new electrical instruments wowed their crowds with renditions of Bach and light opera. Varèse was one of the very few contemporary composers who ever wrote for the theremin, including two in the score for his *Ecuatorial*, alongside wind instruments, percussion, and bass voice, but even he later re-wrote the parts for the more traditionally outfitted ondes martenot.

The familiar tendency of recent years for advertisers to shill the latest music tech hardware with the infinite promise of "any sound imaginable" is already at work in the pages of hobbyist magazines at mid-century. Promotional materials for RCA's commercially-produced theremin called it the "universal musical instrument." Jörg Mager, promoting his Sphärophon, promised "a new epoch of music," going so far as to conjure up the spectre of Shakespeare's *Hamlet*: "there are yet things in music of which our book-learning cannot dream." The Dynatron Ether Minstrel console promised "perfection in sound." In the pages of every magazine, a new musical utopia – and at bargain prices.

Even as they looked up to the stars, the sounds of the future were being domesticated, their utopian promises appropriated by commercial imperatives. The final merger of sci-fi and sales patter was effected at the New York World's Fairs of 1939 and 1964, with the push-button households of the World of Tomorrow, soundtracked by the *beep-swish* of electronic music, and sponsored by General Motors. But this was not always the case. Back when Gernsback penned his very first science-fiction story, the music of the future still had the power to shock and disturb. The future was once a dangerous thing.

1.6 Noise-Sounds

A fight broke out at Rome's Constanzi Theatre on the ninth of March, 1913. From his place at the conductor's podium, the composer Francesco Balila Pratella struggled to guide the orchestra to the end of his *Musica Futuristi* even as cabbages, fennel, and verbal abuse rained down on them from the audience.

A group of the composer's friends, led by the poet and founder of the Italian Futurist movement Filippo Tommaso Marinetti, defended with bared fists and canes. The "bloody battle" that ensued soon descended into farce. Half the orchestra fled for their lives. But for Marinetti the event was a "wonderfully heroic spectacle" and "another victory for Futurism."

In the midst of the tumult, the "intuitive mind" of a young painter named Luigi Russolo "conceived a new art." He called it "the art of noises," a music built of "departments stores' sliding doors, the hubbub of crowds, the different roars of railway stations, iron foundries, textile mills, printing houses, power plants, and subways." He dreamed of concerts encompassing "the infinite variety of noise-sounds." The orchestra of the future would no longer sing; it would roar, clap, whistle, snore, bellow, snort, whisper, grumble, buzz, crack, shuffle, rustle, shout, moan, rattle, and scream. He determined to build a series of noise-making machines – *Intonarumori* – with which to populate that orchestra. "I have conceived," he declared, "the renovation of music through the art of noises."

Italian Futurism had announced its arrival in the pages of the *Gazzetta dell'Emilia* on the fifth of February, 1909. Marinetti's 'Founding and Manifesto of Futurism' was not just a declaration of intent, to "sing the love of danger, the habit of energy and fearlessness"; it was also an exercise in personal myth-making and an origin story worthy of Marvel Comics, complete with a re-birthing sequence in a "maternal ditch." Pratella was an early adherent, meeting Marinetti in August 1910 and publishing the first Futurist manifesto aimed explicitly at musicians very shortly afterwards. Over the next two years, he followed it up with two more before Russolo joined in with his *Art of Noises*.

The response of the press was immediate and unforgiving. In September 1912, the London *Literary Digest* stirred fears of "Futurists breaking out in music" as if it were some nasty sort of skin complaint. In the pages of *The Musical Times*, Futurism was variously damned as "decadent," "ugly eccentricity," and a "deformity of the mind." In Germany, the composer Hans Pfitzner felt moved to publish a tirade of his own. *Futuristengefahr* ('Dangerous Futurism') made it "a moral issue" to protect music from falling into such "chaos."

All of which would point to some considerable level of

notoriety for Russolo and Pratella. Except that none of these articles were even about them. The *Literary Digest*'s panic over a pox of "Futurists" was prompted by a concert of music by Arnold Schoenberg. *The Musical Times* had called Igor Stravinsky "decadent," and Cyril Scott's was the "ugly eccentricity." None of whom had any connection with Marinetti's gang. Scour the anglophone press for contemporary references to Futurism and the overwhelming majority prove to be aimed at composers who professed to have nothing to do with it.

Russolo and Pratella are granted a passing dismissal in the 'Occasional Notes' section of January 1914's *Musical Times* and another one-liner in the same section in June of that year. *The Musical Quarterly*, in a January 1916 report titled 'Futurism: A Series of Negatives', mentions no names but does refer to "specially constructed machines" in a possible reference to Russolo's *intonarumori*. One other reference in that journal notes that Pratella's opera *L'Aviatore Dro* may possibly be worthy of further study one day (but not now, thanks). Another journal, *The Chesterian*, also mentioned Pratella in an article of 1920, but only to deem him insignificant. And that's about it. A few scattered dismissals and a bookmark for further investigation, never to be followed up.

Hans Pfitzner had been moved to write his *Futuristengefahr* after reading a pamphlet by Ferruccio Busoni called *Sketch of a New Aesthetic of Music*. Born in Tuscany, but a Berlin resident since 1896, Busoni was a dazzling pianist and a brilliant promoter of new music, though his own compositions tended to be somewhat conservative. His *New Aesthetic*, however, was a tour-de-force. "Music was born free," it grandly proclaims. He goes on to scorn those "lawgivers" who would bind it in rigid orthodoxies.

The essay proceeds to speak of a need for musical "research," of exploring new forms of notation, new divisions of the octave, and new tuning systems. "Creative power," he wrote, "may be the more readily recognised, the more it shakes itself loose from tradition." Edgard Varèse would pick up a copy of the little book while still a student at the Paris Conservatoire. As soon as he had the chance, he left for Berlin and knocked on Busoni's door to ask for tuition. But for Pfitzner, all such talk was pure "Jules Verne," no more than "futuristic kitsch."

Busoni was no Futurist. He did meet Marinetti some time later, at a Futurist exhibition in Berlin, and he even bought a canvas by the Futurist painter Umberto Boccioni. But in an open letter to Pfitzner he declared himself "far removed" from his agitated former countrymen. "I have never attached myself to a sect," he wrote, in the *Vossische Zeitung* in June 1917. "Futurism ... could have no connection with my arguments."

It is at least possible that Pfitzner's essay had a sinister ulterior motive, with very little to do with musical aesthetics. After all, it was only after the second edition of Busoni's *New Aesthetic* in 1916 that Pfitzner suddenly decided to take umbrage. By that time Europe was in the midst of war and Pfitzner's own opera, *Palestrina*, was on tour through Switzerland as a propaganda effort organised by the German foreign ministry. Could his real intention have been to finger Busoni as a foreign interloper on German soil by association with the artistic propagandists of an enemy power? Certainly there was a belligerent tenor to his words. In a later tract, against the "impotence" of modern music (and against, in particular, the influential critic Paul Bekker), Pfitzner felt moved to blame art's impasse on the machinations of the "international Jewish movement."

In a 2009 book called *Future Tense*, the Canadian historian Roxanne Panchasi describes a curious feeling pervading writing on the future in France from around this time. She calls it "premourning." Whether talking about articles in popular magazines in which the writer has been asked to speculate about the cuisine of 2933, but ends up describing some new "cerebral wave" technology allowing the people of the future to vicariously experience the more vivid gustatory sensations of the past; or about a Jean Renoir short film in which an African explorer from 2028 visits a ruined future Paris to pick over its remains; there persisted, she claims, "a nostalgic longing for French values and cultural phenomena that *had not yet disappeared.*"

Panchasi scarcely mentions music in her book, but the feeling she describes is familiar from contemporary writing on music – and Pfitzner's in particular. "What if we found ourselves on the pinnacle or had already passed the pinnacle?" Pfitzner had asked in his *Futuristengefahr*. "What if the last century or the last century-and-a-half constituted the blossoming of occidental music, the height, the true shining period that will never come again and upon which follows a decay, a decadence, like that after the blossoming of Greek tragedy? My feeling," he continued morosely, "tends far more toward this interpretation." On a similar note, after attending a lecture by the Swiss composer Arthur Honegger about the possibilities for making music with mechanical player-pianos, one *Musical Times* journalist jumped straight to images of "a great bonfire...kindled with Strads and grand pianofortes," picturing all concert-giving administered bureaucratically by wireless from a central office in Geneva.

Today, we tend to look back on those first few decades of the twentieth century as an era of thrusting modernism and violent reaction – Stravinsky's *Rite of Spring*, Schoenberg's "emancipation of the dissonance," the Futurists themselves – but the more one reads reports actually published at the time, the more pervasive seems this sullen feeling of "premourning" and "nostalgic longing."

The real impact of Russolo and Pratella's ideas upon their contemporaries seems to have been quite minimal. What little notoriety they were able to stir up afforded Russolo a few opportunities to demonstrate his noise-machines in public. He met, at different times, with many of the important composers of his age. But for the most part they seemed to do little more than humour him. Stravinsky would later confess that he only "pretended to be enthusiastic." Both Varèse and Maurice Ravel promised at various times to compose new works for the *intonarumori* but neither ever came to anything. Perhaps they were also just pretending.

By the end of the 1920s, Russolo had largely given up on the art of noises, sinking instead into an all-consuming obsession with the mysteries of the occult and fascist politics. Few early twentieth century histories of music mention his name. His ideas might have been forgotten altogether, had they not been taken up, some years later, by one of the most famous American composers of the whole modern age.

1.7 Sound Itself

"I believe that the use of noise to make music will continue and increase until we reach a music produced through the aid of electrical instruments which will make available for musical purposes any and all sounds that can be heard." John Cage's essay 'The Future of Music: Credo' begins in a tone almost as righteous as Marinetti's, were it not that such declarative statements in block capitals are interspersed in the printed text with more whimsical passages in standard capitalisation, as if he were intent on quietly undercutting his own oratory.

First delivered as a talk in Seattle in 1937, the text has since been reprinted numerous times. It is probably the composer's most well-known and widely distributed written statement. But it comes from right at the beginning of Cage's career, long before he composed any of the works he is known for today. In fact, from its opening salvo onwards, Cage's 'Credo' reads in large part like little more than an extended gloss on *The Art of Noises*.

Cage would later place Russolo's manifesto third in a list of the ten books that most influenced the development of his own thought. He claimed the text had been "of great encouragement to me in my work" and was wont to say, of the percussion music he wrote in the 1930s, that it was "really the art of noise and that's what it should be called." There are several passages in his 'Credo' that echo Russolo's manifesto, not least his embrace of the "entire field of sound" and his enthusiasm for new devices with which to produce them, his fascination with the ubiquitousness of noise and openness to its peculiar pleasures. There are even typographical things, like the alternation of block caps and standard capitalisation, which are familiar from Russolo's manifesto.

But where his predecessor might come across as hot-tempered, even bellicose in his tirades against the "passé-ists," his brusque dismissal of Beethoven and Wagner, his constant refrain of we must, must, must; Cage's text, by contrast, is characterised by a more gently disarming manner. He took Russolo's indignant howl of protest and reframed it as serene self-evidence. Trying to dispute with Russolo might well have earned you a bloody nose, but you could probably still walk away thinking the man was an arrogant fool. An argument with Cage, on the other hand, sounds to me like the most confounding of experiences, apt to leave one wandering off, wondering if maybe black *is* white and white black after all.

For all their different temperaments and discursive styles, though, what Cage and Russolo shared was a sense of infinite possibility. In spite of its many refinements and expansions over the preceding centuries, the orchestra simply wasn't good enough for either of them and neither could see any reason why any sound that they could hear or conceive of might not profitably be put to music. There is a utopianism that perhaps we are lacking today, now that the meat of their argument is basically taken for granted.

All the same, it would be a mistake to see here an argument for libertarianism. Russolo speaks very little of freedom in *The Art of Noises*. Surrounded by clamour all around, he determines to "score and regulate harmonically and rhythmically these most varied noises." Faced with sound "gushing confusedly and irregularly," he seeks to "coordinate," "extract," and "select," to "conquer the infinite variety of noise-sounds." He seems more concerned with constraining the noises engirdling him, reigning them in rather than emancipating them.

And so, in 1937, does Cage. In 'The Future of Music' he declares his intention to "capture and control" the sounds of his environment. Any sound can be music, he seems to be saying – just so long as it does what I tell it to. But just a few years later, Cage would have an experience that would change his attitude to music and sound forever.

In the late summer of 1952, John Cage stepped into the anechoic chamber at Harvard University's Psycho-Acoustic Laboratory. An anechoic chamber is a room-within-a-room specially designed to be totally acoustically dead. The structure is externally soundproofed and internally resistant to all sonic reflections. With walls typically covered in jutting cones made of rubberised foam to absorb reverberations like a sponge sucking up water, they tend to look very much like the inside of the rocket ship built by David Bowie's character in *The Man Who Fell to Earth*, as seen on the front cover of the 1976 album *Station to Station*.

The room at the Harvard Psycho-Acoustic Lab was built at the beginning of World War Two in order to provide the best possible environment in which to test pilots' ability to follow commands while subjected to the almost deafening sounds of the complex electronic equipment that surrounded them. During the war they would bring in conscientious objectors to blast them with white noise and bark instructions at them, test their reactions. Later on, anechoic chambers would be used in sensory-deprivation experiments. Some studies have suggested it can take just fifteen minutes in an anechoic room for subjects to start hallucinating. "World War II nearly drowned," Paul N. Edwards writes in his book *The Closed World*, "in the noise of its own technology." The anechoic chamber was a major flank in the struggle to control that noise.

But its effect on John Cage was paradoxical. He was disturbed to find that he could still hear two distinct sounds, even in this soundless space: one high-pitched and one low. Asking the engineers afterwards if there might be a fault in the system, some kind of leak of extraneous noise filtering through somehow, he was informed that the sounds he heard were in fact coming from his own body: the high sound was the operation of his nervous system, the low that of the blood circulating through his veins. Cage had in effect been forced to confront the mechanisms of his body as something alien and exterior. "I was basically a machine," he would say later, "over which I had no intentional control."

Some sense of how much Cage's attitude changed can be obtained from another essay by Cage, also called 'The Future of Music', but written over thirty years after the first one, in 1974. "Anything goes," he says now. What he is now looking forward to is a "nonintentional expressivity... where sounds are sounds and people are people." Cage had been talking about this for some time by this point, "letting sounds be themselves" without anyone controlling them and directing them. Such had been his approach ever since he came out of that anechoic chamber in Harvard.

Confronted with his own body as an alien force, Cage must have felt as powerless to control the sounds he could hear as the subjects in the lab's wartime experiments. Being Cage, he simply went with it and let them be. His work, *4'33"*, for a *tacet* performer in three movements, came immediately afterwards. At the premiere of that piece, in a barn near Woodstock, Cage marvelled at all the different sounds he could hear despite the pianist's unmoving fingers. "You could hear the wind stirring outside during the first movement," he said. "During the second, raindrops began pattering the roof, and during the third the people themselves made all kinds of interesting sounds as they talked or walked out."

Writing in the *New Left Review* in the mid-Sixties, the English composer Michael Parsons accused Cage of a kind of quietism. "He seems to *accept* things as they are," Parsons wrote. "He looks with a sort of wonder at things just because they exist or happen; his attitude to the world is one of perpetual child-like amazement; he seems content to observe things, without any desire to change or influence them." You can see what he means. Later in the decade, Cage would begin publishing extracts from his diaries under the title 'How to Improve the World (You Will Only Make Matters Worse)'. He concludes his 1974 essay on 'The Future of Music' with an anecdote about Henry David Thoreau accidentally setting fire to a forest while broiling some fish and then simply sitting back to enjoy the spectacle. "I think [the story] is relevant to the practice of music in the present world situation," Cage writes, "and it may suggest actions to be taken as we move into the future."

But beyond that, what does it really mean to let sounds be themselves? In 'The Music of the Future', Cage doesn't really elaborate. But in a slightly earlier lecture, delivered at the Music Teachers National Association in Chicago in 1957 and later reprinted in the book *Silence*, he advocates giving up "the desire to control sound...[and] discovering means to let sounds be themselves rather than vehicles for man-made theories or expressions of human sentiments."

There is a suggestion that, left alone, unburdened with "theories" and "human sentiments," sounds might offer up some purer form of truth of their own. It is telling that all of the examples Cage follows this up with – otters along a stream, rain falling, and mists rising – are drawn from nature, as if what Cage really wanted was sounds unaffected by any human influence at all. Douglas Kahn, the author of *Noise, Water, Meat: A History of Sound in the Arts*, has noticed this subtly conservative streak in Cage, his tendency to construct a "musical bulwark" against the teeming sounds of mass culture and the urban environment that had become increasingly pervasive during his lifetime – the very sounds, moreover, that had provided the principal source of inspiration for Luigi Russolo in the first place. *The Art of Noises* imagined combinations of "the sounds of trolleys, autos and other vehicles, and loud crowds." Cage spoke instead of mountains, "the flash of lightning and the sound of thunder" – all tropes familiar from the romantic vision of sublime nature concocted during the nineteenth century.

Where can we go today to find a sound distinct from the effects of human presence? How long will you be able to spend in the wilderness before the roar of an aeroplane passes overhead? You might go to the Arctic Circle and listen to icebergs creaking and groaning as they melt and break apart, but isn't this, too, a product of human industry?

Soviet geologists began referring to our own geological epoch as the "anthropocene" in the 1960s, in order to register the inescapable impact of humans upon the earth's mineral make-up. But we also need to recognise something like an *anthropophonocene*, an age in which no sound exists in a vacuum, unmolested by the work of men.

Cage is just one of many twentieth-century musicians who have framed their practice in terms of a search for some original sonic purity, stripped of "man-made theories or expressions of human sentiments." By recording the sounds of bells and bits of wood, then playing them back on turntables with their initial impact cut off, the French broadcaster Pierre Schaeffer felt himself approaching "direct contact with sound material." He called his experiments *musique concrète* – "concrete music" – because he believed he was not setting out from abstract principles, but proceeding directly from the raw "sound data."

Karlheinz Stockhausen and Herbert Eimert, working in the electronic music studio of the Westdeutcher Rundfunk in the Cologne, had advocated the use of electronic sine tones as a "pure" form of sound, in contradistinction to the grossly "referential" nature of Schaeffer's recorded noises. Eimert, in the very first essay of the first issue of the journal *Die Reihe* that he and Stockhausen edited together, claimed their material was "sound itself," as if the electrical apparatus had provided access to the very atoms of the acoustic universe. Speaking in the same publication, the Belgian composer Karel Goeyvaerts goes further, speaking of "pure vibrations" which stem "from the basic components of sound production."

But at the same time, from quite another direction, Pauline Oliveros would express her disinterest in the kind of "control" sought by both Schaeffer and the Cologne group. Her interest was simply in "sound." When I met Oliveros at the Zentrum für Kunst und Medien in Karlsruhe, she told me about a pivotal early experience with an old-fashioned wire recorder, while taking down her improvisations as a teenager. "The recorder was taking in things that I wasn't," she said to me. It was listening better than she could on her own. Her future direction would be determined by a frank appreciation of the nature of "the sounds that were coming in."

In each case here there is some sense of a sound *beyond* abstract categories, a truer, more organic material. And yet in each case, the discovery of that sound is a product of working with complex – often military – machinery, just like Cage stepping into the anechoic chamber. There is an uncharacteristically pragmatic tone to the latter's second essay on 'The Future of Music'. "People frequently ask me what my definition of music is," he writes. "It is work. That is my conclusion." He speaks simply of a job to be done, without fuss or fanfare. For all their many differences, Schaeffer, Stockhausen, Eimert, and Oliveros share something of this pragmatism, this stance of objective, common-sense activity. The implication is of a music free of myth, as if now the musical grand narratives of the nineteenth century could be dispensed with, and the serious business of dealing with sound itself, on its own terms, could be got on with. But as Claude Lévi-Strauss recognised a long time ago, music *is* myth. They cannot be dissociated.

It was Georges Bataille, writing in a catalogue essay for the 1947 exhibition *La Surréalisme* at the Galerie Maeght in Paris, who noted that "the absence of myth is also a myth." It implied, he believed, a breakdown of communication, a breakdown of society's own self-understanding. It was perhaps "the only *true* myth." For composers in the late twentieth century, it may have been the most powerful myth of all.

1.8 The Alter-Destiny

In the year John Cage delivered his final address on 'The Future of Music' in New York, a man named Sun Ra travelled through time. The force that powered his time machine was music. In a spaceship shaped like a pair of binoculars with a Moog synthesizer at the controls, Ra moved from a far-off planet to 1940s Chicago, into the future, and back to the present day, winding up in Oakland, California. "How do we know you're for real?" asked a teenage girl in rimless glasses and an orange sweater when Sun Ra materialised in platform moon shoes in the middle of her youth club.

"I'm not real," Ra replied with equanimity. "I'm just like you. You don't exist in this society. If you did, your people wouldn't be seeking equal rights. You're not real ... So we're both myths. I do not come to you as reality. I come to you as the myth because that's what black people are: myths."

Space is the Place, the film Sun Ra co-wrote, soundtracked, and starred in that year, is a kaleidoscopic *Gesamtkunstwerk* combining concert footage, wild costumes and dancing, and a surreal narrative involving a cosmic card game, an interstellar employment agency, and the tuning of the universe. Like Charles Fourier before him, Ra was able to combine incisive social critique with visionary sci-fi fantasies in a deliriously potent brew that looked and sounded like nothing before or since. "Sun Ra's flying saucer imagery is about accepting the mystical powers that one knows, culturally, and seeing science as a mystical process as well – a process that has to do not only with deductive reasoning, but with creating power and positing new social myths," Tricia Rose once said, in an interview with Mark Dery.

"If you're going to imagine yourself in the future," she continued, "you have to imagine where you've come from; ancestor worship in black culture is a way of countering a historical erasure." For Sun Ra, the imagination of his own origins began in Rocket City – Huntsville, Alabama, the place where they built the Redstone Rocket – way back in the 1930s.

In 1936, the man then still known as Herman Blount was enrolled on a teacher-training course at a Huntsville college. In music-appreciation classes, he studied the work of far-sighted twentieth-century composers like Arnold Schoenberg and Alexander Scriabin. But at night he travelled the spaceways. In his book *Space is the Place: The Life and Times of Sun Ra*, John Szwed quotes from Ra's diaries of the period: "these space men contacted me. They wanted me to go to outer space with them ... I'd have to go up with no part of my body touching outside of the beam, because if I did, going through different time zones, I wouldn't be able to get that far back. So that's what I did."

In his dreams, Ra was taken to Saturn. "First thing I saw was something like a rail, a long rail of a railroad track coming out of the sky, and landed over there in a vacant lot." Extraterrestrial creatures with "one little antenna on each ear" spoke to him and told him "that when it looked like the world was going into complete chaos, when there was no hope for nothing, then I could speak, but not until then. I would speak, and the world would listen."

Over the years, Blount's personal mythology would evolve with his music. As he moved from the big-band sound of early heroes like Fletcher Henderson and Duke Ellington to something far stranger, forged of electronic whoops and blaring horns in free rhythmic counterpoint, Blount began to tell people that he was himself from Saturn, that his name was Sun Ra, that his musicians were "tone scientists."

His Space Trio of 1952 grew into a sprawling, many-tentacled sinfonia variously called the Myth Science Arkestra, the Solar Myth Arkestra, the Intergalactic Research Arkestra, amongst many other equally fantastic names. Their performances became more and more physical, synaesthetic, and elaborate, ornamented with strange costumes and ritual chanting: "Get off, get off!" – "What stop?" – "Where?" – "Venus!" The different elements of the group slowly began to coalesce into a wholly new kind of performance theatre. Ra called them "myth rituals" or "cosmo dramas." In amongst the chanting and sermonising, the wild dancing and coloured lights, sounded a music at once highly disciplined and thrillingly spontaneous, wrapped up in narratives tracing the history of African-American people from the Egyptian pyramids to a cosmic future.

Long before the modular synthesizer was even invented, Ra knew that electronic music was on its way. He read *Popular Mechanics* magazine and spoke often of coming technologies. When the first wire recorder became available, he got one. When Hammond released the Solovox electronic organ, Ra was an early adopter. He was notable for his interest in the use of technology and studio equipment, had a keen ear for proper microphone placement and recording technique. The equipment he used and the instruments of his band members became ritual objects, endowed with mythic properties. "I can do things with synthesizers," he said to *Downbeat* magazine. "If I want to get the sound of thunder, it's there. If I want the feeling of space, it's there."

As his arsenal of equipment grew, he proved that there was more to the hi-tech future music instruments touted by Hugo

Gernsback's magazines than a quick fad or a new sound with which to play the old classics. A Moog could also be a tool of liberation, a noise-making machine that drew sounds not from the city streets but the depths of the imagination, a means of launching music into outer space. Arkestra members quoted in Szwed's book confirm that space-age imagery and track titles like 'Tapestry from an Asteroid', 'Other Worlds', and 'Music from the World Tomorrow' would encourage them to play more experimentally. "You had to think space. Had to expand beyond the earth plane," trumpeter Phil Cohran explains. "We didn't have any models, so we had to create our own language." Where Russolo had once urged the incorporation of sounds from the new urban environment into his art of noises; Sun Ra went further, demanding sounds not yet synthesised, from worlds not yet glimpsed.

But more importantly, Sun Ra used myths about the future to compensate for a past that had been systematically erased. African people brought to America on slave ships were separated from their parents, lied to about their origins, and would be repeatedly treated as an unwelcome foreign body for generations to come. Fine, said Ra. We *are* aliens – aliens from outer space, from Saturn, or from another galaxy. As he flicked through the pages of *Popular Mechanics* he saw only white faces staring back at him. On the TV news, he saw only white people going to the moon. He could see there was an urgent need for new myths, to bring his people together, to take charge of their own destiny. In Sun Ra's records and performances there was a promise that the world would not be won by strength of arms but by music. All of these themes are glimpsed in *Space is the Place*, the film Ra wanted the whole world to "recognise as a thing of beauty."

They met once, Sun Ra and John Cage. It was June 1986 and they were brought together to perform as a duo by a concert promoter named Rick Russo. Cage had never heard of Ra; Ra "thought he had read" Cage's first book, *Silence*. The results of their meeting make very strange listening: Ra is jamming out florid passages on a brand new Yamaha DX7 digital synthesizer, equal parts free jazz and flying saucer soundtrack, then Cage would chant from his own poetry, staring at his watch the whole time to count out randomly determined periods of silence and activity. Later, Cage would correct a journalist who referred to the two of them playing together. "We did not play *together*," he insisted – merely at the same time.

But perhaps the oddest thing about their meeting was the venue. It was not a concert hall, nor a jazz club, but a sideshow hall in an amusement arcade on Coney Island. They played amongst posters advertising snake charmers and mermaid parades in New York's last actual, literal freak show. It could be seen, in some respects, as an ignominious setting for two of the century's greatest composers. Both of them, by this point, were better known for their supposedly outlandish public pronouncements than their actual music.

Closer in some ways to understanding Sun Ra on the level of both music and mythology was Karlheinz Stockhausen. He gushed to the *Melody Maker* magazine, after seeing Ra play in 1971, that the beginning of the concert was "first-class avant-garde experimental music that you can't put in any box" – even if the latter half was merely "cheap, movie music." But Ra and Stockhausen had something in common. They both came from outer space.

The Stockhausen who saw Sun Ra play in the early Seventies was a very different man to the former *Die Reihe* editor who had advocated total control of the sound atom in the 1950s. Since the late Sixties, his music had embarked on a strange new turn. Now Stockhausen spoke of an "intuitive music" – or what he would later call "music from utopia." One such intuitive composition, consisting of just a few lines of text instructions, begins, "Imagine you are a higher being, which comes from another star..." In the year of his *Melody Maker* interview, he seemed to have done just that.

In a series of "crazy dreams," Stockhausen learnt "that not only did I come from Sirius itself, but that, in fact, I completed my musical education there." As he explained in an interview with Mya Tannenbaum, the discovery led him directly to the composition of a new work called *Sirius*, a fantastical music drama that the composer would dedicate to the "American pioneers on earth and in space."

Sirius opens with a sound familiar to all fans of British science-fiction television: flying saucers coming down to earth via the medium of the frequency-shifted oscillator whirl of an EMS Synthi 100 analogue synthesizer. From these spacecraft descend four soloists, messengers from Sirius here to explain their philosophy of music. The soloists are typically dressed in glittery space disco outfits in the manner of *Night Flight to Venus*-era Boney M. They don't say "Take me to your leader," but we do get a baritone "We greet you, Earthlings" recalling Marvin the Martian, Daffy Duck's extraterrestrial foil from the *Looney Tunes* cartoons. First performed at the opening of the Albert Einstein Spacearium in Washington, D.C., on the fifteenth of July 1976, the work marked a turn in Stockhausen's oeuvre towards music theatre that would find its culmination in the extraordinary week-long epic *Licht*, which occupied the composer continuously from 1977 until 2003.

Over a total of twenty-nine hours of music, *Licht* is scored for choirs of adults and children, several orchestras, African percussion ensembles, multiple soloists, dazzling electronics in eight-channel surround-sound, and – at one point – a string quartet distributed across four different airborne helicopters. The story weaves together elements of the composer's own life with ideas drawn from Judaeo-Christian scripture, Hindu philosophy, Sumerian cults, German folk tales, space-age imagery, and the future of the world. It *may* be the most grandiose, ambitious production of the whole twentieth century. In comparison, the *Star Wars* films sound like a cheap school play. But Stockhausen was far from alone in dreaming grandiose sci-fi dreams in the 1970s.

The Who's Pete Townshend spend the early part of the decade developing a bizarre film-slash-rock opera called *Lifehouse* set in a post-apocalyptic future Britain whose straggling hordes were to be awakened from their deadening slumber by music generated from their own astrological charts. David Bowie and Marc Bolan announced plans for a multimedia collaboration about a future utopian society. Even Don Kirshner, the man behind pre-fab pop group The Monkees, worked on a film about a hip, young beat combo called Toomorrow, drafted in to entertain the inhabitants of an alien civilisation. Of all of these, only the last ever came to fruition (it starred Olivia Newton-John and, to be honest, I cannot wholeheartedly recommend it).

By the end of the decade, with the arrival of punk, such projects quickly started to look ridiculous. The Stranglers declared that there were 'No More Heroes'. The Sex Pistols sailed down the River Thames screaming "No future." It may seem improbable, but punk helped to usher in a new kind of realism, a new artistic pragmatism that spoke of individual empowerment rather than collective transcendence. Groups as different as Heaven 17, Public Image Ltd., and Sigue Sigue Sputnik, all made up of former punks, styled themselves as mini-media conglomerates, demystifying the corporate pop machine. Like F.T. Marinetti's 'Founding and Manifesto of Futurism', seventy years earlier, the cry spread that "mythology and the mystic ideal are defeated at last."

1.9 Network Realism

In the winter of 2013, I finally found a composer willing to respond to my question about the music of the future. I was living in Paris at the time, in a little fifth-floor attic apartment in the fourteenth arrondissement. I remember catching the metro on my own out to the *banlieue* and walking for some fifteen minutes through near-deserted streets. Eventually I came to a tall glass door on a narrow side street, quite devoid of any other signs of life. Through the door and up the stairs, I found myself in Le Cube, a digital arts centre that any English city would be proud of. Everything about it seemed bright and modern. Even the wallpaper was augmented with scannable icons capable of launching dedicated web-browser windows. I have a friend who has worked for several years in a library just down the road from Le Cube and he had never heard of the place.

I had come to see a performance by the Tennessee-born artist Holly Herndon. She was billed as part of a digital arts festival called Némo. I had been intrigued by Herndon ever since her name came up in a Skype conversation I had with the artist and writer James Bridle earlier that same year. We'd been talking about something called "network realism," a concept he summed up as "an attempt to articulate what it feels like to live in a time when very, very distant things – distant in space and distant in time – are made visible and immediate by the network." Having a background in publishing, Bridle cited things like fan fiction and the novels of William Gibson as examples of kinds of stories that exist at least in part by virtue of that connectivity, of life lived as part of a global system of linked computers. When I asked him about music, he brought up Holly Herndon as someone whose work and ideas *"feel* to me like how we're approaching working with the network." He wouldn't be drawn much further on the subject at the time. "Music isn't really my sphere," he protested. So ever since, I'd been on the lookout for an excuse to talk to Herndon herself. Then along came Festival Némo and Herndon's headline performance.

The theatre at Le Cube is a big black box. Herndon, also dressed in black, stepped up to her laptop. "Hello," in sans serif, appeared projected on the wall behind her. She picked up a mic and started singing long, wordless vowel sounds, tapping instructions into her computer as she did so. Her voice multiplied in layers, building up into a shimmering choral harmony then breaking down into crystalline digital fragments, stuttering and choking in rhythmic bursts. A cascade of electronic beats dropped, her voice's many virtual reflections splintered into shifting melodic patterns in counterpoint with the drums. Throughout the gig, I was struck by the sense of acrobatic motion to the sounds she used. They seemed to burst out of the speakers unexpectedly, plunging the listener into different intensive folds. From time to time, I'd notice her stroking what looked like Walkman earbuds across the surface of her computer.

"They're induction mics," she explained to me when we sat down to talk after the show. "They pick up electrical activity." By rubbing them across the frame of her laptop she was picking up otherwise hidden signals from the black box, bringing the oblique interior to the surface. "I'm giving it a voice," she said.

Herndon was pretty tired when we met in Issy-les-Moulineaux. She was coming to the end of a week-long European tour and the previous night's gig in Utrecht had turned into a late one. Between sentences, she would fork mouthfuls of the dinner she hadn't had time to eat before the gig. So she masticated her meze as we chewed over the implications of making music with computers. "The thing that I think is most different," she said, slathering hummus over a little pink sausage, "is that the laptop mediates my relationships and my emotional well-being, which other instruments don't do. Half of my life is mediated through that machine."

A few months before, I had been at the Palais de Tokyo, a major art centre in Paris, to interview Conrad Shawcross, who had just installed a sixteen-foot-tall tack-welding robot in its basement. The British artist had programmed this giant mechanical arm to gambol and gyre through a series of toroidal sweeps and arc-like swoops. He had also invited several different composers to write music for his machine choreography. Holly Herndon was one of them. The seven-minute piece she came up with flits between great waves of oceanic resonance and sudden reports of spasmodic digital scree. Though some of the sounds involved may recall the hissing, gurgling, and rustling evoked in Luigi Russolo's *Art of Noises,* the feel of the piece is a million miles from the kind of Futurist noise music of the early twentieth century.

"I'm not a chauvinist, racist man for one thing," Herndon said when I brought this up, "so it's gonna sound a little bit different. But one thing that I'm really adamant about is this 1960s *Jetsons* idea of the future that a lot of people still kind of get stuck with... I mean, come on! Let's fantasise about what the next kind of future aesthetic is."

"There's so much more that we can do," she continued. "Laptops are way stronger than they used to be. I couldn't do my live set on my last laptop. It melted down. And the internet really is dramatically changing music. One of the great things about audio is you can be really responsive and really *fast.* Almost like *South Park* –something'll be in the news and then the next week they'll reference it in the show. You can't do that with *vinyl.* No way. But you *can* do that with online music. A lot of hip-hop can be like that sometimes. I also think that the way that we're consuming music is no longer in these album formats, because of iPods and online listening. We're hearing jammed-up sounds next to each other. John Cage right next to Rihanna right next to *whatever* and it's like a *cluster jam* that I think is having an aesthetic impact."

What kind of aesthetic impact do you see that having in the future? I asked.

"I see 2014 being full of a lot of hard abrupt edges, a lot of fast changes. It's like a collaging of spaces – and that really is in direct reference to web browsers and online experience. All these different worlds jammed up right next to each other. Do you remember that show *Quantum Leap?*"

Of course, I said. I was a big fan of *Quantum Leap.* But on the web, *Quantum Leap* is almost an everyday experience now.

"Yeah," she said, "but it's hyper-*Quantum Leap.* Like, he's *constantly* jumping."

Herndon's image reminded me of one of the classic works of Nineties net.art. The narrative of Olia Lialina's *My Boyfriend*

Came Back from the War unfolds through boxes of text and lo-res images in an increasingly subdivided browser window. As you click on different phrases or pictures, you are led down different paths, affecting the way the tale progresses. Your attention leaps from one box to the next, a picture slowly emerging through the disjuncture of manifold lines and threads. It's a simple but very elegantly designed work in which multiple story strands and time frames co-exist on the screen at any one time. It's also a very moving, quietly tragic piece of narrative.

I started to wonder what *My Boyfriend Came Back from the War* would be like as a piece of music. As it turned out, the Irish composer, Jennifer Walshe, had actually created a work based directly on it – only Walshe's *Olia Lialina's M.B.C.B.F.T.W. (Redux, at Rest)* re-imagines the original as a completely silent film, composed entirely of differently coloured post-it notes, variously stuck to and peeled from a square, beige-coloured frame.

I first discovered Walshe's Lialina tribute on YouTube. She may be one of the few composers in the contemporary classical music world with her own YouTube channel. It is fitting somehow, since over the last few years Walshe, like Herndon, has been using her music as a means of thinking through the cultural consequences of the internet. In the spring of 2015, she decided to open up the conversation and ask her friends on Facebook, framing the question around the art-world term "post-internet."

The "post-internet" idea first came to prominence on Gene McHugh's blog of the same name in 2009–10. For McHugh, post-internet could mean art that was made with a built-in awareness that it would be shared online (whether you like it or not), art made literally *just after* spending time surfing the web, and/or a situation where the net is "less a novelty and more a banality." Contemporary with McHugh, artists like Marisa Olson, Oliver Laric, Brad Troemel (aka The Jogging), and others set about making video, sculptural, and photographic works in response to this condition, with all its wild and sometimes messy implications.

But by the end of 2014, the art world was starting to turn against the idea. *Art in America*'s Brian Droitcour had warned of 'The Perils of Post-Internet Art' in October 2014, calling the phrase "embarrassing to say out loud." In *Artforum*, a month later, the term was labelled "problematic," while in *Art Review* it was called simply "strange." Only a few months into 2015, *Art Monthly*'s

Morgan Quaintance was declaring the "end of post-internet art," which, "like the death of grunge," he saw as a "development that should be celebrated."

Meanwhile, Walshe was paying attention – but from a slight remove. "It's sort of awesome," she told me when we spoke over Skype a little later in the year, "because there's a massive argument going on and you're not a part of it. So all of the internecine feuds that are going on in art over whether post-internet is ruining everything, you can just stand back and it's not really such a problematic thing." Still the world of new music seemed baffled by it. "I posted something on Facebook," Walshe recalled, "and what I realised quickly was that a lot of people didn't really seem to understand the term. A lot of composers were not really sure what was it all about."

We were talking in the run-up to her performance at 2015's London Contemporary Music Festival where Walshe was to perform a recent work called *The Total Mountain*. "If you've ever felt like watching someone in a glamour wig singing the text of Twitter posts about Katy Perry's links to the Illuminati in the full-throated style of classical opera, then Jennifer Walshe may be just the composer for you," I wrote at the time, in an article for the music website *Thump*.

"*The Total Mountain*," I continued, "is a forty-minute video and performance piece. It chops together YouTube clips with screengrabs of Wikipedia pages, text messages from an ancient manuscript with selections from the Department of Homeland Security's flagged-words list. It's got One Direction, lots of swearing, doge, Valley Girl accents, and the aforementioned Twitter opera." The work had received its premiere, the previous year, at the world's oldest contemporary music festival, in Donaueschingen. I can't quite imagine how it was received there. Even at the LCMF, where it came sandwiched between the gleeful global hypercolour pop of Felicita and Neele Hülcker's experiments with the sound-induced tingling sensations of autonomous sensory meridian response, some people were still clearly left baffled by the piece ("That was a bit much," another composer of my acquaintance said to me on his way out of the hall). But what was undeniable was that *The Total Mountain* had been composed entirely of elements that would be immediately recognisable to anyone plugged into the media reality of that particular moment in time – yet completely alien to anyone who had managed to sleep through the previous five or ten years.

But it will probably also look just as strange to a perfect amnesiac five or ten years in the future. In an essay published in the journal *Musik Texte*, Walshe is quick to point out that the aesthetics of a piece like *The Total Mountain* may be about the "*current* iteration of the internet," but that the internet itself is "constantly changing."

"The internet," she writes, "doesn't know what it means yet." Which makes this the perfect time to start inventing it.

In a time of uncertainty, fabricate. In the absence of history, write mythology. For the last seven years, Walshe has been collating the *Historical Documents of the Irish Avant-Garde*. It's a huge project, bringing together works stretching back to the 1830s and up to the 1980s, gathering within its purview such diverse figures as the fin-de-siècle occultist Andrew Hunt, whose ritualistic "automatic music-making" employed objects such as kettles, gramophones, and typewriters; or the Guinness Dadaists, who wrote sound poetry in Gaelic and fought with the Republicans in the Irish Civil War; or Pádraig Mac Giolla Mhuire, whose outsider folk music prefigured the long tones of La Monte Young and other American minimalists. What all of these previously forgotten figures of Irish artistic history have in common is that they are all completely fictional, carefully fabricated by Walshe and a small group of collaborators as a liberating exercise in alter-ego aesthetic production.

The project took shape in 2009, at a time when Walshe was living in New York and working a lot with Tony Conrad. In the early Sixties, Conrad had been a key member of La Monte Young's seminal drone-based group, the Theatre of Eternal Music, but has been left frustrated by Young's persistent refusal to release any of the recordings from that period of the group's development. "There are a lot of recordings that Tony played on and La Monte is sitting on them," Walshe said in an interview with Louise Gray for *Musicworks* magazine. "Tony said to me, 'It's kinda crazy that we can't hear them!' and I said," dropping to a conspiratorial whisper, "what if I claim that the Irish invented minimalism? And he said, 'Yeah!'"

The many books, films, and recordings since created by Walshe on behalf of her spurious forebears make up a formidable archive

– probably the closest thing I've found to the "evidence" brought back by Ray Bradbury's Time Traveller in 'The Toynbee Convector'. Walshe may not be showing us music from the future, but she does prove that there is still room in the twenty-first century for a different relationship with history, for the creation of new mythologies. As she writes on the "Aisteach" website dedicated to the project, it's an exercise in "what if?" An invitation to dream.

For a long time, my favourite page on Wikipedia has been the 'List of Hoaxes on Wikipedia'. Partly I love it because it's such a great trove of funny stories, like the student who made himself mayor of a fictional Chinese town, or the guy who invented a spurious 1970s children's TV series about a cat with magical powers and later claimed it had been dubbed into French by Serge Gainsbourg. There are also loads of fake bands and musical instruments (one of my favourites is the one about Digital Lady, a San Francisco rock band from the hippie era with albums called *Lush Bum* and *Impeccable Creams*, who supposedly used kitchen utensils to imitate the sound of a Moog synthesiser).

The other reason I like this page is because it reminds me of a story by Jorge Luis Borges called 'Tlön, Uqbar, Orbis Tertius'. The tale begins with Borges being introduced to an encyclopaedia entry about a non-existent place called Uqbar. "One memorable feature," Borges notes of this entry, concerns the literature of Uqbar, which "never referred to reality but rather to the two imaginary realms of Mle'khnas and Tlön." A little later, the eleventh volume of another encyclopaedia, dedicated entirely to the spurious world of Tlön, comes into his possession. Ultimately, the whole story opens up into a sort of conspiracy about a secret society who determine to invent a country, and later a whole world. But then a strange thing starts to happen.

Borges notes that the idealist philosophy of the people of Tlön influenced somewhat the reality of the place. Lost objects would sometimes be found twice by two different people in two different places, the duplicate being called an instance of *hrönir*. Sometimes entire archeological digs could produce fabulous artefacts from nothing more than the hope of the diggers. By the end of the tale, objects from Tlön, obeying the impossible physics of Tlön, have begun to appear on Earth – a compass inscribed in one of its alphabets, an impossibly heavy coin. Finally, word of Tlön starts to spread, bewitching people everywhere. The languages and science of Tlön are taught in schools. Its history replaces our history. "Contact with Tlön, the *habit* of Tlön, has disintegrated this world."

A fake entry about a fake country in a real encyclopaedia, an entirely fake encyclopaedia about a planet that exists only in the fiction of that fake country, gradually, over centuries, succeeds in transforming the real world. There are streets – even whole towns – that are invented by cartographers in order to mark out their maps as their own, to trap those who would copy them. Agloe, a hamlet north of Roscoe in upstate New York, was created for just that purpose by Otto G. Lindberg of General Drafting Co. It was a paper town, a copyright trap, with no physical existence. But today, Agloe is real. People live there. People have started businesses, fallen in love, and been born there. Maybe great works of art have been made there or will be made there soon. Drawn by a misleading map reference, people moved out and built lives. A falsified past created a new and unpredictable future.

Interval: 2014

It was almost three in the morning. Ten thousand people were standing in the mud with their hands in the air. A scrawny little man with NHS specs and a lopsided undercut stood on top of a pair of CD decks mounted on a fifteen-foot salvage-punk spaceship and told everyone to "get low." A score of lime-green lasers transected the sky, spiralling wildly, incandescently. Smoke enfiladed the crowd in bloated plumes. Jets of multi-coloured flame shot up from the footlights. On a screen at the back, Geiger-esque vector graphic aliens twerked feverishly.

Skrillex had been on stage at France's Eurockéenes Festival for a little over an hour, bass flowing from his touch like ectoplasm from the fingers of a medium, a heaving scrum of compacted human bodies writhing in blissful abandon. Everything was kicking off. A visitor from a century ago would truly have thought himself a witness to some baroque vision of hell.

Not that the musical life of a hundred years ago was any stranger to excess. In 1914, Paris had just witnessed Stravinsky's *Rite of Spring* with its multiple tonal centres, juddering dynamic leaps, and manic overlapping rhythms so confounding even the Ballets Russes found it hard to dance in time. Charles Ives was working on his *Universe Symphony* for multiple orchestras spread across the hills and valleys, painting in sound the very origins of matter. Richard Strauss had recently leapt from the high modernism of *Elektra* to the high camp of *Der Rosenkavalier*, while his *Alpine Symphony* called for one hundred and twenty-five musicians and lasts an uninterrupted fifty minutes. The Russian composer Alexander Nikolayevich Scriabin, meanwhile, continued to struggle with his *Mysterium*, a work he considered so powerful that it would bring about the end of the world.

For the musicologist Richard Taruskin the avant-garde of this period "is perhaps best characterised as *maximalism*." The turn of the century, he writes, was a period in which the "acceleration of stylistic innovation" became "so marked as to seem not just a matter of degree but one of actual kind."

Taruskin points to the extension of musical lengths into "awe-inspiring mountains," to the vast amplification of volume and resources, to a dramatic increase in the acceptance of dissonance and its suspension, to a "saturation … with significant motifs to be kaleidoscopically recombined" such that "the musical texture was made ever more pregnant with meaning."

These were the contours of maximalism at the last fin-de-siècle. Few would argue that Skrillex's 'Scary Monsters and Nice Sprites' is exactly "pregnant with meaning", but we may nonetheless start to recognise a like work of supererogation amongst some of the leading lights of our own never-ending end-of-days. Saturation, amplification, kaleidoscopic recombination. The specifics have changed, but we can recognise the general shape.

For instance, a couple of months before my trip to Eurockéenes, Michigan-born techno DJ Seth Troxler wrote an editorial for *Thump*, in which he complained that the dance music scene is "so flooded... you get it all on a platter up-front. Lasers! LED screens! Pyrotechnics! DROPS! CAKE IN YOUR FUCKING FACE!" Troxler did not approve. "That's not clubbing," he insisted, "that's a concert of cunts." The article ended with a plug for something called the "Big Titty Surprise Party" being hosted by Troxler himself in Barcelona.

It's hard to avoid a certain air of snobbery in Troxler's tirade. When he claims that the very same action – the example he gives is "a girl doing lines of coke off another girl's naked vagina" – could stand for "freedom" at Berlin's notoriously exclusive Berghain club, but mere "trash" at the Ultra Music Festival, isn't he just appealing to the elitism of the techno purist? Like, sure, go ahead, shed your underwear in a public place and dowse your nether regions in class-A drugs for all to partake of – but do make sure you're doing it in the *right* public place, with the *right sort of people*, wearing *the right sort of clothes*. Say what you like about big music festivals, but I've never heard of one refusing admittance to anyone for sporting the wrong shoes.

Inheritor to a strange utopian tradition stretching back to the medieval carnival, there has always been something distinctly Rabelaisian about the modern music festival. Wandering about the rain-sodden byways of the Eurockéenes site, in amongst banners proclaiming the festival's promotional slogan ("Music in Paradise"), I saw a whole menagerie of novelty onesies; people with writing on their faces drinking from colostomy bags; a crowdsurfing reveller in a latex horse's head; a cardboard sign triumphantly held aloft with "FUCK HER RIGHT IN THE PUSSY" in crudely marker-penned block caps.

I stumbled through rivers of slurry pockmarked by discarded

tampons and leery-looking men offering "free hugs"; past fat
white men in shorts breakdancing ineptly in the mud before a
group of jeering onlookers; another man, topless and sunburnt,
staggering through the crowd with vomit streaming continuously
from his gaping maw.

All of which is somehow normal, par for the course in this
heterotopian mirrorworld. The average festival field paints a
picture worthy of Bruegel.

But the festival is also a site where one stall amidst the burger
bars and panini stops can pledge its "Solidarity with Burkina
Faso"; where a vast anonymous crowd can suddenly feel at one,
united in melancholy by the defeat of the French football team
and the equally melancholic, universalist pop music of Stromae;
where striking technical staff are given time on the main stage
to say their piece and connect their complaint over changes to
benefit structures in recent French legislation with anti-austerity
protests across Europe. "Our struggle," they boomed through the
colossal festival PA, "is your struggle."

Half a century ago, the Russian literary critic Mikhail Bakhtin
recognised in the medieval institution of carnival the creation
of "a second world and a second life outside officialdom" in
which hierarchies are overturned and everything, for a brief
moment, is permissible. Central to Bakhtin's analysis is the
formulation of a certain kind of bodily and material excess,
grotesque overindulgence, and "brimming-over abundance."
But for Troxler, the mud and the cake and the energy-packed-
extremes of the festival are a distraction and a betrayal of the
original purity of the Paradise Garage and authentic club culture.
Just "trash" without the mystical "something more" celebrated
in dance music's hallowed temples.

Minimalism has always been the preserve of an elite. Furniture
by Starck or Conran; gleaming office blocks and apartment
complexes by Mies van der Rohe and his many imitators.
There is no minimalism in a slum. Shanty towns are invariably
characterised by a bricolaged aesthetic of teeming incongruities.
Everything in heaps, spilling out everywhere. And perhaps it
was in the slums of the world's cities – or rather in the colourful
appropriation of the image of the slum by artists like Diplo
and MIA – that we might seek the origin of the contemporary

revolt against minimalism.

One hour before Skrillex began, MIA had strutted onto the second stage at Eurockéenes. She came accompanied by dancers, hype people, and flanked by two giant neon snowflakes, each one riddled with filigreed arabesques like an Uzbek temple recreated on Blackpool pier. Maya Arulpragasam's global hypercolour dancehall is voracious in its magpie tendencies, freely appropriating from reggaeton, baile funk, dubstep, and son in the service of a bustling international style, intertwining global ghettoes and hip urban labels.

In 2007, the year of MIA's biggest hit, the award-winning multi-platinum 'Paper Planes', lifestyle blogger Charlotte Rivers published the book *Maximalism: The Graphic Design of Decadence & Excess*. "After years of minimalist rule," she wrote, "graphic design has seen a return to a more decorative, maximalist approach. Ornament is no longer a crime." Rivers applauded work like Michael Nash Associates' designs for John Galliano, the "legendary" *Visionaire* magazine, and Takashi Murakami's encrustation of Louis Vuitton handbags with diamonds and cartoon characters. Collectively, for Rivers, such examples ushered in a new era of decoration, sensuality, luxury, and fantasy. And in the midst of it all, MIA, like a brash cheerleader for a movement without motto or unity. The video to 'Paper Planes', with its ringing cash registers and exploding cartridges, sees Arulpragasam serving hot sandwiches from a market stall winnebago. The record itself sounds equally stuffed with highly spiced and heterogenous ingredients.

But in the design world, the term was then already old, familiar at least since Aurora Cuito had "been so bold", in a book for Loft Publications in 2002, as to apply the label to the likes of Alsop and Stormer's Peckham Library, Ettore Sottsass's Olabuenaga House in Maui, and numerous buildings by Zaha Hadid and Eric Owen Moss. What both Cuito and Rivers' publications share is a prefatory assertion that minimalism and maximalism are opposing tendencies that have forever oscillated back and forth in some never-ending and seemingly inevitable historical cycle. But this is to posit a false equivalence.

Everybody knows what minimalism is – in music, especially, there are well-defined and historically bracketed minimalist schools in classical music (mostly in New York in the Sixties and

Seventies but also in California from the late Fifties) and techno (mostly in Berlin and Cologne in the Nineties). Maximalism is another matter. You can count the number of English books with that word in the title on one hand, while minimalism's volumes surpass triple figures. In fact, no-one spoke about maximalism at all until long after minimalism had been codified and institutionalised (Taruskin's comments on Stravinsky, Strauss, and so on, were retrospective, written only in 2010). Even then it never really caught on.

The art critic Robert Pincus-Witten may have some claim to precedence here. "I'm repeatedly being fingered to pull together an exhibition of all the truly innovative artists including the young Italians from all the stables," he wrote in *Arts Magazine* in 1981. "If I do it, I'll call it Maximalism to make as strong a differentiation from the indurated and academised sensibility Minimalism of the Seventies as possible." He would later admit that it was "a shock-value journalistic term," but he did regret that it had so much of a "harder time" gaining acceptance than his previous coinage, 'postminimalism,' which he regarded as part of the same continuum.

Part of the problem was that many of the stylistic tropes (ornament, kitsch, appropriation) and several of the artists (David Salle, Julian Schnabel) that Pincus-Witten had hoped to dub "maximalist" were very shortly to be subsumed under the all-conquering rubric of postmodernism, a term that Pincus-Witten seems to have regarded as some sort of commie conspiracy. So despite one gallery show of mostly neo-expressionist artists in New Jersey in 1983 and a single follow-up essay in the winter 1986 issue of *Effects*, "maximalism," as a figure of critical discourse, was largely stillborn.

But in the twelve years since Cuito's book of maximalist buildings, the word has started cropping up all over the place, inventing its own history as it goes. Notably, three years ago, in several reviews of Rustie's album *Glass Swords.*

"Rustie most reminds me, not of rave per se so much as a certain kind of rave-inspired dance maximalism," wrote Mark Fisher in *The Wire*. "*Glass Swords* recalls the managed overload of Basement Jaxx, Daft Punk's *Discovery*, or – reaching even further back – 808 State. What it has in common with these three precursors is the ambition to produce a dance music that can compete with – and outdo – rock at its most maximalist, with electronic flatulence, spiralling synths and digital excrescences replacing bass and guitar."

Fisher was not alone. Reviews in *Dummy*, *Pitchfork*, and *Discobelle* followed suit. And a little later, so too did *Spin*, *Village Voice*, and *The Guardian*. As Simon Reynolds would sum up in *Pitchfork*, part of the vogue stemmed from the word itself being "vague and capacious enough to contain a whole bunch of ideas and associations." But he did find sufficient coherence in the sheer density of inputs ("in terms of influences and source,") and outputs ("density, scale, structural convolution, and sheer majesty") to connect Rustie's debut with scores of other maximalists, from the jazz fusion of Weather Report to the more contemporary psychedelic sounds of Gang Gang Dance, Flying Lotus, and James Ferraro.

For Reynolds the excesses of the present are a by-product of technology, whether the infinite possibilities of digital music software or "the endless upgrades in audio-video entertainment, from high-definition flatscreen TV to CGI-saturated movies and 3D cinema to the ever-more real-seeming unreality of games." *Glass Swords*, he claimed, evoked "the euphoria of gliding frictionlessly across the datascape." To find out how the maximal virus has mutated since Reynolds's essay, then, it makes sense to delve deep into the datascape itself.

For some time now such digital dumpster-diving has been the vocation of Adam Harper, a writer and blogger who has spent the past few years scouring the morass of SoundCloud and Bandcamp pages in search of the "new online underground" and exhibiting its tastiest morsels in a series of columns for *Dummy*, *Electronic Beats*, and *Fader*. In one such excavation from the summer of 2013, Harper arrayed the "neon" sounds of net label Donky Pitch alongside more overground material by Hyetal, Ikonika, and Sophie.

Harper was suspicious of calling all this stuff "maximalism" even if he did grant that it is somewhat "thicker-textured and more formally active than some classic dance styles." But there was something in his description of the Sophie track, 'Bipp' – "rhythmic architecture … deceptive bulk … blobs of curved muscle … wave upon peristaltic wave" – that recalls the "grotesque realism" favoured by Mikhail Bakhtin.

Performances by Sophie, Rustie, and Ikonika are not generally known for their laser shows and general extra-musical hoo ha. There is no cake in your face. But there is a feeling of exuberant extravagance to the music itself. If their tracks rarely leap totally into the unknown, they do push all the excesses of dub, rave, synth pop, J-pop, and computer game chip tunes to such an extreme that the cumulative effect almost becomes qualitative. A difference of degree threatens to become a difference of type. It is in this sense that we can compare them to the likes of Strauss, Scriabin, and Prokofiev.

Richard Taruskin was ultimately fairly critical of his pre-war maximalists. They were, he claimed, a mere "radical intensification of means toward accepted or traditional ends." Arguably the same could be said of our contemporary audio gluttons. Today's maximalism could be seen as just an acceleration of the twentieth-century project of streamlining, instrumentalising – and, ultimately, weaponising – music's seductive charms. For Taruskin, modernism proper didn't get started until a bit later, when the nineteenth century's yen for "emotional expression," "sensuality," and "religious awe in the presence of the sublime" could finally be put aside. Might our own era's maximal bent then be a like prelude to some great flowering, a sort of clearing of the stage before the entrance of the twenty-first century's very own Varèse?

I rather suspect that a lot of the gnawing suspicion reserved for maximalist musicians and maximalism generally derives from a concern that all that bluster must be overcompensating for something, that beneath all the hyperbole little remains of any substance. There's clearly something ridiculous about performances by MIA and Skrillex. The affected grandeur, the posturing. The former's set at Eurockéenes, in particular, felt at times as much like a fashion parade as a concert. It would be easy to dismiss both as little more than hollow charade. But there remains something seductive about the level of sheer excess on display – as much in the music itself, as in all the other aspects, the lights, the video screens, the costumes, machines, and pyrotechnics, all of which adds to the overwhelming, delirious effect. That very excess is part of what I love about opera. That need for everything at once, to create a whole world on stage. Maximalism at its best can stretch the limits of what's possible, can seem indistinguishable from magic.

The Eurockéenes festival itself, too, though draped in corporate sponsorship and dubious rhetoric, nonetheless managed to retain something of that utopian impulse glimpsed by Bakhtin in the medieval carnival. The sense of everyday norms suspended is palpable (in, perhaps, both a good way and a bad way). To paraphrase Michel Foucault, such spaces can act as a critique and counterweight to the prevailing culture, even as they emphasise and re-assert it. Real spaces that are simultaneously "nowhere." Places of universal communion and ecstatic togetherness, that are also exclusionary enclaves, walled-off gardens for the privileged and the footloose. But I will never forget that feeling of a heaving thousands-strong crowd, drenched by the pouring rain, yet blissful in shared awe and mutual sympathy, as a young Belgian singer-rapper-producer-performer named Stromae took over the main stage on the Friday night.

By the end of my weekend at Eurockéenes I had come to divide the artists I'd seen between the "real" and the "fake." Skrillex and MIA, of course, were decidedly—even defiantly – on the side of the fake. Likewise, looking back, Strauss, Schnabel, and Frank Zappa (the subject of a 2005 book subtitled *The Secret History of Maximalism*) are clearly all great fakers.

But what of *real* music? At Eurockéenes we saw Robert Plant's *Later-With-Joolz*-friendly worldbeat-dadrock, the meticulously recreated Seventies psych of Temples, and the plodding meat-and-potatoes tradrock of The Black Keys.

Of course, I favoured the fake every time.

Second Act: 1852

2.1. Musica Ricercata

One day in July 1952, György Ligeti was standing on the platform of an S-Bahn station in East Berlin, waiting for a train. It was only thanks to an administrative cock-up that he was even in town. He was supposed to be going on holiday. But an incorrectly filed report had mistakenly sent the composer off with a party of factory workers to the Baltic coast. On the way back home to Budapest, they stopped off in the divided former German capital. In the morning, he slipped out of the hotel, made it to the station by foot, and bought a ticket. If he boarded, he could escape to the West – probably even make it to England, where an uncle could have found him a job at a print works. For Ligeti, at that moment, boarding that train would mean freedom.

Six years earlier, Ligeti had welcomed the end of World War Two and the beginning of Hungarian communism with what he would later recall to his biographer Richard Steinmetz as "a euphoric hope for a better future." Both his father and younger brother had died in Nazi concentration camps, his home city was in ruins, and Ligeti himself had only narrowly escaped deportation to Siberia when Russian forces wrested control of Hungary. But as the war ended he found himself accepted into the Franz Liszt Academy of Music. There was, for a few years, this efflorescence in Hungarian musical life. The legendary German conductor Otto Klemperer had taken charge of the state opera. There were frequent performances of the major progressive works of Béla Bartók. After the privations of wartime, the country seemed to be opening up to the world again. It would not last long.

In January 1948, at the All Union Congress of Composers in Moscow, the Soviet chairman Andrei Zhdanov had castigated the supposedly "formalist" tendencies of musicians including Dmitri Shostakovich and Sergei Prokofiev. "It is clear," Zhdanov said, "that a serious spring-cleaning is needed." In the same year, paintings by Picasso were removed from the Budapest Museum of Art. Books suspected of a corrupting Western decadence – such scurrilous tracts as *Don Quixote* and *Winnie the Pooh* – were taken from libraries and bookshops throughout Hungary. Like many of his generation, Ligeti increasingly found his musical energies funnelled into folklore research. His more daring, modernist music was consigned to a desk drawer with little hope of performance. He was also falling in love with a young psychologist named Vera Spitz whose once well-to-do family were threatened with deportation to the countryside, to work off their bourgeois sins.

All these things were on Ligeti's mind as he stood at that S-Bahn platform and awaited his train. Tears sprung to his eyes and he began to shiver uncontrollably. The train came. He did not board. It left without him. He trudged back to the hotel and, ultimately, to Budapest.

Upon returning home, he returned also to a composition for solo piano that he had been tinkering away at since the previous year. "It was then that I first conceived the idea of a static, self-contained music without either development or traditional rhythmic configurations," he told Steinmetz. That work, *Musica Ricercata*, would finally consist of eleven short pieces, radically stripped back: the first contains only one note – until the last few seconds when another is introduced – the second has only three notes, the third four, and so on. The intention was nothing less than "to build up a new kind of music starting from nothing."

To listen to the piece today is to encounter a creeping sensation of being trapped in an inexorable spiral with no way forwards, much as Ligeti himself must have felt upon returning, dejectedly, to the Hungarian People's Republic. A note above the score instructs the performer to play "*mesto, rigido e ceremoniale*" – sad, rigid, and ceremonial. In places, the pianist seems to be stabbing at the keyboard, bluntly and insistently, with just one finger at a time. Ligeti himself referred to the piece as "a knife in Stalin's heart." No wonder it works so powerfully in the Stanley Kubrick film, *Eyes Wide Shut*, about a man trapped in a deadly labyrinth of his own desires. Ligeti finished composing the piece in 1953 and placed it in his desk drawer. It would not see a performance for another decade and a half.

He finally caught the train west, out of Hungary and out of the Eastern Bloc, at the end of 1956. This time his destination would be Vienna, not London. And he would end up not at a print works, but a radio station. The final straw had been the failure of new leader Imre Nagy's attempted liberalisation of the country, when Russian tanks rolled into Budapest on November fourth of that year and closed down all hope of reform. Later in life, one of Ligeti's most vivid memories would be emerging from his basement shelter in the midst of the Soviet siege to listen to a broadcast of Karlheinz Stockhausen's pioneering electronic works *Kontakte* and *Gesang der Jünglinge*, punctuated by the sound of gunfire from the streets outside.

Having escaped, aided in his flight by a conspiracy of railway employees, Ligeti would soon find himself amongst Stockhausen's circle in Cologne, working at the electronic music studios of the Westdeutscher Rundfunk. Galvanised by the dynamic thought of his German contemporary, and by the new soundworld opened up by electronic sound generation, Ligeti set about returning to that vision of a perfectly "static, self-contained" music he had nurtured at the beginning of the decade in that long-suppressed suite of piano pieces, *Musica Ricercata*. What had been proscribed as formalist decadence in Stalinist Hungary was warmly embraced in the West. A succession of brilliant compositions, quite unlike anything composed by anyone before, helped his rise to prominence as a celebrated composer in his own right. Never before had stasis sounded so seductive.

Such was his burgeoning renown that in 1961 Ligeti was invited to the prestigious European Forum, held in the small Tyrolean village of Alpbach. Begun in 1945, at the close of World War Two, by the brothers Otto and Fritz Molden of the Austrian resistance group 05, the European Forum was intended as an interdisciplinary symposium for thinking about the future of Europe. It would come to be highly influential upon the development of the continent's burgeoning federalist project. But in 1961, the theme of the conference was not monetary policy or the free movement of people, but 'Science in the Future'.

Various artists, academics, researchers, and thinkers were invited to contribute short lectures on their views regarding the prospects for their particular discipline. Ligeti had "grave doubts," about the appointment, as he recalled in a 1972 interview, "because what can, in fact, be said about the future? However knowledgeable one is, there is only one thing which is certain, and that is that the future will be something completely different from one's prophecy." Nevertheless, he agreed to the lecture on the condition that he was free to do whatever he liked. It is an interesting caveat, suggesting either a certain bloodymindedness or a clear determination that one's ability to articulate a future for one's art be conditional upon its absolute liberty. In the event, however, he would have nothing to say at all.

When the time came, he stepped up to the podium, set his stopwatch for the allotted ten minutes, and proceeded to stand there, in total silence, before an increasingly restive crowd. It didn't take long for the audience to start booing and stamping their feet. Ligeti responded with equanimity. He elected to direct these noises as if they were orchestral instruments. "Crescendo," he wrote on the blackboard behind him, and "Più forte." Was he composing or simply goading? After just eight minutes, a number of impromptu "soloists" approached the stage to have their taciturn speaker removed, convinced that he had already taken up several times the ten minutes allocated him. Time, evidently, had begun to slow down.

György Ligeti clearly failed to articulate a clear vision of the future on that summer day in Alpbach. But the lecture is now included in the composer's official catalogue of works as a "collective composition" under the title 'The Future of Music'. By so listing the event, is Ligeti just affirming what he said in that interview from 1972, that any attempt at forecasting is doomed to frustration? Or is there a more nuanced lesson to be drawn, that the future is not to be dictated by any figure of authority – a lecturer at his podium, for instance, or a think tank off in a mountain resort – but something collectively negotiated, only finding its truth in the struggle between authority and its others?

When it is spoken of at all by commenters on his oeuvre, the work is generally described as a sort of conceptualist prank, part of a craze for "happenings" that was then beginning to make its way out of trendy universities and New York lofts into art galleries, festivals, and outraged tabloid leader columns throughout the world. But it is rarely asked why Ligeti had found it so difficult to speak on this subject – nor why a composer would be asked to do so in the first place. To answer these questions it will be necessary to go back some three-quarters of a century further, to another train journey and another passenger, who had little choice but to get on board.

2.2 The Acceleration Waltz

The train left Venice at eighteen minutes past two p.m. on Friday the sixteenth of February, 1883. The station had been closed to the public by the railway authorities out of respect for the passenger for whom the train had been chartered. That passenger was a dead man. His name was Richard Wagner.

At the time of his death Wagner was probably the most famous composer in the world – and this in an era when artists were accorded an esteem in society far in excess of what they receive today. By the beginning of the First World War, there would be more books written about Wagner than any other individual bar Napoleon and Jesus.

As his funeral train passed through different towns along its route, mourners lined the platforms bearing flowers and torches. Entering Bavaria, a message of condolences was brought from the king. In Munich the train waited for an hour as people flocked to catch a glimpse of the composer of *The Ring, Parsifal,* and *Tristan und Isolde.* It was almost midnight on Saturday when it reached its final destination: Bayreuth.

Wagner had first pulled into Bayreuth train station some twelve years earlier, in the spring of 1871. That was when he settled upon the town as the location for a specially-constructed theatre to showcase his works. Open since 1853, the train line itself was one of the reasons behind his choice, since it placed the town strategically within reach of both Munich, the home of his patron King Ludwig II, and Berlin, seat of the Prussian throne he hoped to impress. Brick-built and unfussily shed-like in appearance, to some people the theatre he built there even looked like a train station. Certainly, it looked very little like the prevailing fashion for opera houses at the time, as exemplified by the almost contemporary Palais Garnier in Paris, a real rococo gateau of a building, bedecked in neoclassical columns and ornate gilded statues.

Though still quite new, rail travel had already begun to play a significant part in the history of music. Transporting audiences, orchestras, and instruments from place to place, country to country, it facilitated the development of a new mass audience for music, eager to dance to the Viennese waltz or take in one of the fashionable promenade concerts at Vauxhall Pleasure

Gardens. Something like the brass-band competitions held at London's Crystal Palace, to which several thousand competitors and spectators travelled hundreds of miles, would have been practically inconceivable without trains to get them all there. And though the fare presented at the Bayreuth *festspielhaus* had little in common with this new "*popular* music" (as it was called at the time), the economic and technical bases were getting remarkably similar: at least part-funded by tickets and public subscription, linked by the rail networks, and brought to life by electric lighting and dramatic smoke effects (which, at Bayreuth, were actually created by a railway engineer with an old locomotive engine in the wings).

Major music publishers, like Maurice Schlesinger, founder of the French *Gazette musicale* (and Wagner's employer for a brief time in 1840s Paris), would also speculate on rail stocks on the side. In a sense, music had become something like a speculative business itself, since musicians were forced to become ever-more entrepreneurial as the revenues available from court patronage dried up. In his 2004 book about the economics of music in the eighteenth and nineteenth centuries, Frederic Scherer noted a three-fold increase in the number of composers acting as impresarios from the 1700s to the 1800s, often risking their own money to hire a hall, pay musicians, and court publicity, in the hope of high returns that weren't always forthcoming. To cover the shortfall they would take freelance commissions that increasingly served less to flatter some prince than trumpet some technical or infrastructural advance.

Though train travel gave him nightmares, Hector Berlioz managed to compose a 'Chant des chemins de fer' commissioned for the opening of a new station at Lille in 1846. Its lyrics hymned the new mode of transport for making "the future greater, more beautiful." Johann Strauss, whose hugely popular Strauss-Kapelle Orchestra toured all over Europe by rail, composed an 'Eisenbahn-Lust Walzer' ('Railway Desire Waltz') to celebrate the opening of Austria's first line of track. His two sons, Eduard and Johann Jr., followed suit with their own polkas dedicated to the pleasures of train travel, alongside paeans to other technological marvels, like the electric telegraph and a revving engine.

But the railways were not just a source of finance, a means of picking up some of the pennies from the speculative frenzy ballooning around the tracks; they were also a source of genuine inspiration. There is a kind of wide-eyed wonder and tally-ho enthusiasm to the Strausses' train pieces. Listen to 'Bahn Frei!' or one of his other technologically-inclined pieces like the 'Elektro-Magnetisches' polka, with its oddly motorik rhythms and leaping sparks of glissando violins. Johann Strauss Jr.'s 'Accelerationen-Walzer', composed in 1860 for a ball thrown by Vienna University's engineering students, would take its lead from a motor accelerating, becoming one of the first pieces of music to try and directly imitate the sound of machinery.

Many composers also found themselves able – or perhaps compelled – to write their music during rail journeys. Travel was becoming more frequent and train carriages were a lot steadier for putting lines on staves than a horse-drawn carriage bumbling down a dirt track. Giacomo Meyerbeer, the doyen of grand opera in France, a composer whose works were often regarded by critics as much in terms of engineering as aesthetics, is said to have loved writing music on long train journeys. Wagner himself is known to have begun composition of the overtures to both *Lohengrin* and the *Meistersinger von Nürnberg* on the train. You can almost hear the clattering rhythm of wheels against track beneath the strident brass and whirling strings of that last-named prelude. Friedrich Nietzsche felt it contained "something manifold, formless, and inexhaustible ... over-rich in future."

In his book about the history of science fiction, *Trillion Year Spree*, the British author Brian Aldiss would even credit the railways with inspiring the birth of a speculative, future-oriented fiction. The society that produced *Frankenstein*, Aldiss believed, was one in a state of future shock from recent demonstrations in Britain of the new steam locomotive. "Because it has the power to move itself. Because it is the first thing on land ever to move faster than a cheetah, a stag, a galloping horse," writes Aldiss. "Because it brings us into a world of timetables, where we have to conform to a thing's convenience, not it to ours. Because the timetables induce us to look ahead to the material world stretching like the endless plain before us."

More precisely than ever before, trains articulated a journey from A to B that already was promising the moon. In the fantastic literature of the period, fictional astronauts were no longer transported into space by angels, celestial chariots, or migrating flocks of geese; engines now carried our imagination to the stars. As the tracks spread across Europe, a succession of fictional spacefarers employed smoke-bellowing machines to journey to the moon, inspired by the speed and unswervable trajectories of the railway lines. Trains had come along like a physical manifestation of the new century's forward thrust, its headlong drive into the future. And music was along for the ride.

In 1844, the illustrator J.J. Grandville opened his science-fictional fantasia, *Un autre monde*, with a steam-powered orchestra playing a 'Concert Mécano-Métronomique'. His vivid drawing depicts a band of blackened pumps and pistons in humanoid form playing saxhorns and cellos. The accompanying programme note offers a selection opening with the overture from the (fictional) opera *Les Rails-Notes* and closing with the (equally spurious) symphony 'La Locomotive'. Presented to a bewildered French public less than a year after the Paris-to-Orléans train line became the first sizeable length of track in the country, *Un autre monde* offers a panoramic tour of the industrial imagination. It takes in visions of animals waltzing in human masks, great cast-iron bridges linking the planets, museums that display the art of the future alongside that of the past, and all manner of aerial locomotions and post-human transformations. But in this vision of anthropomorphic engines hitting the high notes of *Les Rail-Notes*, Grandville oneirically anticipated, by just a few decades, the smoke bellowing out by a train boiler to cover the scene changes at Bayreuth's first *Ring* cycle.

Wagner's funeral train was more than just a convenient way to move a corpse. It was the final link in a symbolic chain, enclosing the composer, his music, and its popular association with technical and aesthetic progress (whether positively or negatively appraised). By the late nineteenth century, a fondness for Wagner was considered as accurate a barometer of a person's modernity as might be an interest in evolutionary theory, possession of a dinner jacket, or a passion for Theosophy. To the many onlookers who watched it pass or greeted its arrival, it seemed fitting that his body was brought to Bayreuth by train, a mode of transport only introduced during his lifetime, for exactly the same reason that witnesses of a later era found it natural to see the bodies of Princess Diana and the Queen Mother paraded upon horse-drawn carriages. The latter drew their legitimacy from their link to the past and their cortège was chosen to emphasise that. But Wagner, at least in the popular eye, was a man of the future. And if there was one thing that nineteenth-century audiences were hungry for, it was the future.

2.3 Zukunftsmusik

By the time of his death, Richard Wagner was indelibly associated in the public mind with one particular phrase – *Zukunftsmusik*, "the music of the future." But it was not his own. The phrase had been thrust upon him quite against his own protestations. And, like a precocious example of the Barbra Streisand effect, the more he protested, the more the phrase persisted.

There is a – most probably apocryphal – story that, after one of the first performances of Wagner's opera *Lohengrin* in Weimar in 1850, an animated discussion of its merits broke out between the work's conductor, Franz Liszt; Liszt's girlfriend, the Russian princess Carolyn zu Sayn-Wittgenstein; and the critic, Franz Brendel, editor of the *Neue Zeitschrift für Musik*. Brendel, ever the stuffed shirt, was convinced that *Lohengrin* was too daring in its musical language for present audiences to take. "Very well," the princess declared, "we are creating the music of the future." Somehow it stuck. Supposedly.

Flush with the renown he earned as a boy virtuoso, convinced of his own manifest destiny as a sort of artist-priest sent from heaven to lead the faithless to the musical promised land, Liszt used the cushy (if rather ill-paid) role he had landed as Weimar court conductor to promote a very specific vision of a music renewed, as he liked to put it, "through the spirit of poetry." To that end, he set about building up his own repertoire of what he considered to be the most advanced-sounding music of the day – principally his own symphonic poems, along with the operas of Berlioz and Wagner.

Liszt was, by all accounts, an extraordinary fantasist and a brazen self-publicist. He liked to write autobiographical essays in which characters from Byron poems would converse and flirt with him. He was the pseudonymous subject of at least two actual novels. If Carly Simon had been around in the 1840s, that song probably really would have been about him. But he had a visionary streak when it came to music. He believed it spoke in a "mysterious language" directly to the dream-life of objects. So Liszt went around *Zukunftsmusik*-ing to anyone who cared to listen – much to the consternation of conservatives of all stripes. It made good copy and he knew it. More than that, he believed it.

But Wagner wasn't having any truck with it. He never seems to have entertained this story, of the princess's quip to Brendel, as the true source of the phrase that would soon haunt his every write-up. He was convinced that the whole notion of a "music of the future" was an act of spite on the part of *Rheinische Musik-Zeitung* editor, Ludwig Bischoff. "A music, forsooth," as Wagner wrote bitterly, "which would haply sound quite well in course of time, however ill it might sound just now." This slander, Wagner presumed his friend Liszt had then taken on in what he took to be a "clever stroke," comparable to the actions of the Dutch Calvinist nobles during the Eighty Years War. The Calvinists, called "beggars" (*gueux*) by the ruling Spanish court, re-appropriated that name and made it their own (much as, later, the Fauve and Impressionist groups of artists would name themselves after terms used in hostile reviews – in Dutch, such an act of re-claiming is now known as *geuzennaam*).

Neither of these competing origin stories for the *Zukunftsmusik* meme are really convincing. Liszt was a notorious self-mythologiser, and this particular story comes from a famously unreliable biography written during his lifetime (and under his supervision). Even the composer himself admitted (or boasted?) that this book was "more to be invented than to be written after the fact."

Wagner's suspicions about Ludwig Bischoff, on the other hand, can probably be chalked up to the nefarious paranoia about Jewish conspiracies that was apt to ruinously consume Wagner in the years of his exile, following his part in the failed Dresden uprising of 1849. Whether or not Walter Benjamin was right when he perceived a failed revolution behind every fascism, in Wagner's case at least, it seems to hold true. In the April of 1849, he was a revolutionary; by September of 1850, he was an anti-semite.

None of which is to excuse anything. But what I would like to suggest is that the idea of a "music of the future" had, by the 1850s, become *necessary*. Wagner was always to some extent the patsy for ideas of uncertain origin. Those ideas exerted a powerful influence on the subsequent path of cultural history. If he did not exist, somebody would probably have had to invent him (and, in fact, at no point did the mere fact of Wagner's actual existence ever stop anyone from inventing him, again, and again, and again).

Either way, as Franz Brendel would later recognise, by the end of the 1850s, the very term *Zukunftsmusik* had become a "party slogan." It was a phrase that seemed to divide the musical life of the mid-nineteenth century in twain. On the one side: Liszt and his disciples at Weimar, the composers Joachim Raff, Peter Cornelius, and Hans von Bülow, and the critics, Richard Pohl and Franz Brendel; all self-conscious, self-admitted "*Zukunftsmusikers.*" They believed.

Allied alongside them in the public mind – no matter how reluctantly at times – were Berlioz and Wagner, at least in part by dint of their operas making up so much of the Weimar performance repertoire.

On the other side: Liszt's former concertmaster, the violinist Joseph Joachim, and the young Johannes Brahms. Both of whom were signatories to a notorious manifesto published in the *Berliner Musik-Zeitung Echo* on the sixth of May, 1860. Then there was Brahms' close friend, Clara Schumann, who nonetheless refrained from signing this letter to the *Echo*. And, with them, the Viennese critic, Eduard Hanslick.

What was called "the war of the romantics" was a battle fought on two fronts. In 1854, Hanslick published his *Vom Musikalisch-Schönen* (*On the Musically Beautiful*), a staunch defence of music's autonomy as no more than "form moving in sound." He presented the musical work as a kind of ideal object, engaged in a play of immanent "beauty" quite independent of any actual or potential listener. The expression of meaning, for Hanslick, was "superfluous," a "chimera," and quite irrelevant to the specificity of music's formal beauty. Immune to emotion, devoid of all sense, and radically separate from all the other arts, music, for Hanslick, was to refer only to itself. To inspire thoughts, feelings, or actions was not the job of music. It should simply sit there, sounding pretty.

If Hanslick named few names in 1854, *On the Musically Beautiful*'s second edition, four years later, singled out Liszt's symphonic poems and Wagner's aesthetic essays as particularly egregious. Against their impassioned lyricism, Hanslick proffered an aesthetics based – however vaguely – upon the "methods of the natural sciences" as if his career depended on it. Which in fact it did, since after Vienna's student revolts in 1848, the Austrian Ministry of Education looked to the cool detachment of scientific objectivity to reinforce a harmonious never-ending present. Any suggestion of idealism was enough to arouse suspicions of sympathy for the student radicals. In its place, absolute objectivity, measurable quantities, and enduring truths were considered the path to social harmony. Music's meaninglessness was practically state policy.

As a lecturer at the University of Vienna, Hanslick could not afford to be anything but dispassionate. But his apparent objectivism acted as mule for a creeping backdoor idealism. When music means nothing and expresses nothing, the only guarantor left for the ineffable "beauty" Hanslick goes on about, is the work's dubious state as a product of some even more ineffable "human spirit." Between his first edition of 1854 and the second of 1858, Hanslick did what he could to bury this. Gone were references to music as an image of the "infinite" or "the great motions of the universe." But what remained was this discursive gap between the ear seduced by beauty and the mind analysing form. Richard Pohl, Weimar's critic-in-residence, once sarcastically suggested that if music is just a play of sounding forms, then surely we will one day see an automatic "composing machine" that any child could use to produce music the equal of Mozart's. When finally, in the twentieth century, people really did create machines that could produce music sounding at least superficially like Mozart, the composers who used them were apt to justify their creations in terms remarkably similar to Hanslick's.

Meanwhile, Brahms and Joachim canvassed half of Germany for signatures to their letter to the *Echo*. They finally succeeded in corralling just four: their own, plus those of a school music teacher called Bernhard Scholz, and Brahms's best friend, a man named Julius Otto Grimm. For these four, the very notion of a "music of the future" was offensive. They felt it their duty to roundly condemn *a priori* all "new and unheard-of theories." The very idea, they felt, "was contrary to the innermost spirit of music." Wagner, for his part, referred to the authors as a "musical temperance society."

That the sole name singled out in this manifesto was Franz

Brendel's has led some to assume that the whole affair was little more than a petty squabble over lingering resentments that the *Neue Zeitschrift für Musik*, the journal founded by Brahms's friend and early champion, Robert Schumann, had passed into the hands of an editor attached to the Weimar school. The irony being that Schumann's plan on establishing the *Zeitschrift* in the first place had been to champion precisely the kind of music infused by poetry that Liszt had subsequently made his slogan and the very standard of futurist music.

But it is a mistake to regard the "war of the romantics" as a mere "extension of biography," as Liszt's twentieth century biographer Alan Walker does. What was at stake was nothing less than the possibility of music meaning something, and being committed to something. This was a fight over the very possibility of the *new* arriving in music. In a Germany still reeling from a domino rally of revolutions and counter-revolutions, *new* could mean only one thing.

2.4 A Dream If Ever There Was

It's worth remembering that the whole notion of the *future* – of the future, that is, as a space of hope and projection, as something that might be radically different to the present – was itself still fairly new in the 1860 of Brahms and Joachim's manifesto. Practically all the associations that this word has for us today did not exist in the middle of the nineteenth century. There was none of today's industry of anticipation. None of the think tanks and trend forecasters. Hugo Gernsback had not yet coined the phrase "science fiction." F.T. Marinetti had not published his *Manifesto of Futurism*. Jules Verne hadn't written a single novel and H.G. Wells wasn't even born.

There were utopias, sure. We can find projects for ideal states and cities in the sky as far back as Plato and Aristophanes, probably earlier. Since Thomas More's *Utopia* of 1516 there had been plenty: Evandria and Oceana, Arcadia and Christianopolis, Wolfaria and Antangil, endless cities of the sun, of gold, and of happiness. Every few years a new republic of the imagination. But such fictional places were separated from their author's homeland by space, not time. There was no travelling into the future; more likely, a voyage at sea, a storm, a shipwreck, and an uncharted island with peculiarly expository natives.

There were a few exceptions: a six-page pamphlet of 1644 with the title *Aulicus His Dream, of the King's Sudden Coming to London*, in which the author, a Presbyterian rector and soon-to-be chaplain in Cromwell's New Model Army, panics about the possible imminent return of King Charles. Two thick volumes of 1659, *Épigone, histoire du siècle futur*, amounted to a fairly standard chivalric epic which just happened to be set many years after it was written, against the background of a now vastly expanded French empire. There was an epistolary novel in 1733 called *Memoirs of the Twentieth Century*, in which a diplomat supposedly of the late 1990s bemoans the expansion of papal influence but reports an otherwise largely unchanged world. Finally, *The Reign of George VI, 1900–1925*, was a fantasy in which the succession of Hanoverian Georges that ruled England for much of the author's eighteenth century continued ad infinitum into the nineteenth and twentieth with evermore bloody effect.

What all these tales had in common was a total blindness to the possibility of real, material change. The same technology, the same political structures, the same social norms persisted no matter how far ahead the author looked. The future for these writers was rather like the exotic locales used by certain popular novelists of the mid-twentieth century: little more than a colourful backdrop, vaguely sketched in, before which the same old plot tropes could play themselves out unaffected.

György Lukács, the Marxist intellectual (and – briefly – minister to that 1956 reformist socialist government in Hungary, whose failure led immediately to Ligeti's flight to Austria) would write something similar about historical fiction before the nineteenth century. "Not only the psychology of the characters, but the manners depicted are entirely those of the writer's own day... What is lacking," Lukács continued, "is precisely the specifically historical, that is, derivation of the individuality of characters from the historical peculiarity of their age." All that was about to change.

The specifically futuristic would step onto the literary stage in 1771 with Louis-Sébastien Mercier's *L'an 2440, rêve s'il en fut jamais*, a book soon after translated into English (only slightly inaccurately) as *Memoirs of the Year Two Thousand Five Hundred.*

In fact, Mercier's vision of the year 2440 went through four English translations and two American editions, as well as being translated into Dutch and German, within the author's lifetime. Which is lucky – since it was immediately banned in Mercier's native France, leaving him forced to have it printed across the border in Amsterdam before ferreting it back into the country in secret. What did the censors of a still-feudal France find so threatening about a book framed from start to finish as a dream? It said that the world would change. For an *ancien régime* whose whole legitimacy was predicated on its timeless permanence, nothing could be more seditious.

Mercier may have been inspired, in part, by a series of articles published in the *Mercure de France* while Mercier was still a precocious teenager. Beginning in July 1755, they purported to be the collected papers of a society of men of letters, submitted to the newspaper from the year 2355. These learned gentlemen from the twenty-fourth century had supposedly sifted through what remained of the cultural artefacts of the eighteenth century in order to discern the traces of former ages through the analysis of "our French antiquities."

But beneath the conceit of future art criticism, the anonymous author (believed to be the king's own arts administrator, Charles-Nicolas Cochin) was relatively free to poke fun at the mores of his own time and insinuate scurrilously about the poor tastes of his superiors. It is not long after the standard Enlightenment-era flattery to the reigning monarch, for instance, that the author proceeds to curse the reign of Louis xv as a "time of delirium" and a "corrupted century." The combination was evidently popular, because after an initial run of three articles looking back from the future at eighteenth-century architecture, Cochin returned in 1756 for two further series on painting and sculpture.

At a time when most music existed only in the necessarily limited run of hand-written manuscript copies, and old works were rarely revived on the concert stage, being most often replaced by the new in a regular succession, Cochin quite naturally failed to imagine that sufficient music from the eighteenth century would survive into the twenty-fourth to provide for its own dedicated series of reports. Eighteenth-century composers didn't think like that, with one eye on their legacy. Since most music still wasn't printed or published and there was little in the way of copyright to protect a work's author once it was out in the world, they generally had no more thought for any posthumous reverence that might be attached to their work than you do of your weekly shopping lists. They fulfil a particular purpose at a particular time for a particular group of people. And that, for the most part, was all.

Cochin's narrator does, however, speak quite extensively about the Paris Opéra, though our critic of the future is reticent to believe that such a paltry theatre could possibly have provided for the musical needs of all the people belonging to a city like Paris. The author can only hypothesise that "the music of this time was very simple…[and therefore] didn't inspire in them this delicious sensation that it stirs in us, now that it has been brought to perfection." These few lines may be the earliest example of a kind of musical futurism. Under the wings of a satire intended to prick the present, a speculative musicology creeps in with utopian designs.

Like Cochin, Mercier would use the imagined impeccability of the future's music to critique the musical institutions of his own time. His protagonist in *L'an 2440*, upon dreaming his way to the Paris of the twenty-fifth century, is soon escorted to the theatre. "Are we at the opera?" he asks as the curtain rises and the symphony strikes up, "this music is sublime." His guide assures him that they have reserved from the "monstrous" opera of the eighteenth century only the good, reviving in the process, "the alliance of poetry and music that was formed by the ancients."

Cochin and Mercier alike were the beneficiaries of an unprecedented boom in the business of publishing, which, since the beginning of the century, had become increasingly professionalised. In Britain, the circulation of newspapers rose eightfold between 1712 and 1757. There were then three times as many novels published in 1790 as in 1750. Across the Channel, the situation was complicated by the combination of a rigorous censorship with a policy of manufacturing large quantities of paper for export. This had the effect that France found itself in the position of depending economically on the production of books in Switzerland and the Netherlands that had been banned at home. They were presumably well aware that their neighbours were only printing so many books on the expectation that a significant number would be smuggled back across the border into France. The royal court may have been perfectly sincere in their belief that certain texts were dangerous and needed banning, but still, they needed the tax income from the paper trade.

Inevitably this had the effect of weakening the monopoly held by the French state over the control of time. Political predictions had been explicitly outlawed by Henri III in 1579, during the wars of religion. Later, Louis XIV would crack down even harder on astrologers and freelance prophets of all kinds under the pretext of an edict demanding the incarceration of the insane. But things, evidently, were slipping. A gap was opening up offering new opportunities for parties interested in defining and steering towards the future. It would be eagerly exploited by a buoyant print industry.

2.5 The Classics

Few industries benefited more from the expansion in publishing than music. Hampered for four centuries by the ill-match of musical notation and Gutenberg's movable type, a series of innovations – both technical and commercial – began to produce a vast expansion of printed music towards the turn of the nineteenth century. It would have far-reaching consequences for the whole art form's sense of self-definition.

Though today we may trace the birth of printed music to a fifteenth-century hymn book, known as the *Constance Gradual* and produced in 1473, certain inherent difficulties in printing partition left the practice fiddly, cumbersome, and enormously variable in quality and legibility. Apart from anything else, for a long time music printers were never really sure who their market was. In the eighteenth century, however, several factors conspired to make the process a more attractive commercial prospect.

The slow relaxation of censorial control from both the church and the court, its not-so-subtle undermining from abroad, and the tacit acceptance of that by the state – all that certainly helped. As did the appearance, first of all in Paris but soon copied elsewhere in Europe, of dedicated music shops, where musicians could hang out around a clavichord and try out the latest works. With the development of the piano into an increasingly efficient and compact domestic orchestra-substitute, a new form of "house music" created new audiences for sheet music. The practice of engraving on copper plates – later zinc or pewter – enormously increased the quality and consistency of prints. Most significant of all perhaps, was the invention, at the very end of the century, of lithography. The product of a Prague-born actor and playwright named Alois Senefelder, lithography was a new method of printing with etched limestone which proved much better suited to printing the fiddly overlapping detail of musical scores. That it was launched in Vienna at the very height of the *Wiener Klassik* would appear, in retrospect, an auspicious conjunction.

Born a generation apart, the respective musics of Ludwig van Beethoven and Johann Strauss Sr. can be regarded, in certain respects, as equal and opposite reactions to much the same set of circumstances. Beethoven moved to Vienna from Bonn in the last decade of the eighteenth century, Strauss was born there in the first decade of the nineteenth, just one year after Senefelder established his lithography business there and set about revolutionising music publishing. Both composers would have found themselves in a city that, having had virtually no music publishing industry just a few decades before, was suddenly one of the business's very few world centres. They were also amongst the first generation of composers who had to rely on this trade for their income. Beethoven's diaries, in particular, are riddled with the minutiae of extracting coin from recalcitrant publishers. Knowing that a work's full value might well be realised long after its first performance, he began to think about the music he was composing in a different way. His later works, in particular, are quite clearly written not just for present purposes.

With a rapidly expanding music business, music shops with well-stuffed shelves on the high street, and an explosion of reprinted works by long-dead, supposedly forgotten composers, it must have seemed to the two of them as though they had access, for the first time ever, to the whole history of recorded music at their fingertips. Their respective responses to this sudden plenitude were about as different as can be imagined.

It was Wagner who would later divine, in Beethoven's symphonies, the ghosts of every dance form of the eighteenth century transcended. Stripped of their vulgar functionality, Beethoven raised the figures of the gavotte and minuet to a new, "higher" synthesis in which the rhythms are there to be recognised but not necessarily to inspire physical movement. Had he done the same thing two hundred years later, people would have called it postmodern.

For Strauss, whose career began playing violin in the back room of a pub, the aim was the contrary: to extract from the music of the past precisely those elements that made it popular, lively, and danceable. In a manner analogous to the way, many years later, producer and hit-maker Pete Waterman would turn years of experience as a northern soul DJ towards creating the new form of dance pop that would dominate the British charts in the late 1980s, Strauss transmuted all the crowd-pleasing turns necessary for a bar-room entertainer into the new dance form of the Viennese waltz. It was accorded, in its time, scarcely more respect than that granted by serious rock heads to Kylie's 'I Should Be So Lucky'.

But Strauss's Viennese waltz was more than just a new form of popular dance music. Shocking at first to high-minded observers for the physical proximity of its dancers and the mechanical frenzy of its rhythms; unabashedly commercial; catering to an urban, middlebrow, leisure-time audience; and serving no religious or secular ritual function; Strauss's music represented a whole new way of looking at music. Derisively dubbed *Unterhaltungsmusik* ("entertainment music") at first by the German-speaking press, they would soon follow the lead of the anglophone world in preferring the term "popular music." With this phrase, a new hierarchy of taste was established which would survive virtually unchallenged almost to the present time. There was classical music which was old and serious, and there was popular music which was new but frivolous. Such was the frame of reference established by the burgeoning music press.

But the new popular music was not a purely socio-cultural category. It harboured elements of a distinct style that made it immediately identifiable. Traits that were already recognised as belonging to the Viennese waltz such as the dominance of rhythm over harmony or the "pushed" note before the first beat of the bar remain as salient a century or more later in much jazz, rock, funk, and hip hop. The popularity of medleys, *pot pourris*, and pastiches of every kind made the new pop of the nineteenth century as omnivorous as a box turtle, initiating a cut-and-paste aesthetic almost unthinkable without the growth spurt in music publishing in the previous decades. This explosion of the contemporary in all its liveliness was founded and conditioned upon a changed relationship with the archive.

The music press, at least as far as something regularly produced with a relatively wide circulation, was brand new at this time. It developed as an outgrowth of publishers' printed catalogues, slowly expanding to include reviews and other notices. The press brought with it a whole new language with which to speak about music – basically, the language of romanticism: of *genius* and *great works*, of *high art*, the *classic* and the *classical*. In 1801, the Leipzig publisher Breitkopf und Härtel began issuing their deluxe editions of the complete works of Mozart and Haydn (prototypes, if you like, of today's multi-CD box sets): two thirds of a Holy Trinity of great dead white men to which Beethoven was very shortly added – becoming, in effect, the first composer to be awarded a solemn posthumous reverence *while he was still alive.*

But if, in retrospect, we can see the whole idea of a *classical* music as a largely commercial affair, brought about by a rapidly expanding publishing industry eager to exploit its back catalogue, it should also be clear that it was the result of relatively short-termist thinking. After all, with only a fairly limited amount of old music available to be printed, only a few greats to be ever-more canonised, there are only so many times you can repackage that Mozart best-of. As the nineteenth century wore on, a kind of stultification began to set in. How many times could any self-respecting music writer proclaim Felix Mendelssohn to be the new Bach? Or Rossini the new Mozart? There was a need for new ideas and a new vocabulary for talking about new music.

Into this deficit, at the very end of the 1840s, landed a slender book called *Der Kunstwerk der Zukunft* (*The Artwork of the Future*). Its author was Richard Wagner. Judging by the response it provoked, it would seem few people actually read it. This is not entirely surprising. It is an almost unbearable text to read: pompous, bloated, and fussily argued. But the title alone was enough to spark something off. Music had already invented its own history. It was about to invent as well its future.

2.6 The Arsonists Themselves

Up until the 1840s, Richard Wagner was interested primarily in his position. He wanted to compose operas, in a style somewhere between the French grand opera of Meyerbeer and the German romanticism of Carl Maria von Weber. He wanted to escape his creditors and the debts that dogged him for most of his life. He wanted respect. But most of all he wanted to find a *place* in a highly competitive operatic scene that must have seemed at times like a closed shop, dominated by a small number of established elite players. In the final tumultuous years of that decade, his horizons would begin to expand. He set his sights no longer on gaining territory for himself *now*, but on the future. His own future, yes; but also the future of his art, and the future of mankind. The change in his thinking would coincide with a moment when the composer had direct access to a printing press of his own.

Wagner arrived in Dresden in 1842 after several dispiriting years in Paris, mostly spent writing piano reductions of popular Italian opera numbers for ready money, trying—and failing—to get his own music performed. The Saxon capital promised a job, performance opportunities, and the chance to return home. He was born in nearby Leipzig in 1813, but he went to school in Dresden. It was there, aged nine, that he had witnessed Weber conducting his opera *Der Freischütz*. The experience had been life-changing.

From the start of his term as conductor at the Dresden court theatre, Wagner was a divisive figure. Whenever he altered the orchestra's seating plan or asked for extra rehearsal time, people accused him of making a fuss and changing things around just for the sake of it. But his performances proved popular. He got bums on seats and the orchestra sounded better than ever. So there wasn't much his critics could do. Still, Wagner bristled at the feeling of being watched over by pettifogging provincials.

In the middle years of the decade, a double whammy of failed harvests led to food shortages, rising prices, and general unrest. In 1847 there were bread riots. In February 1848 revolution broke out in Paris. The tumult proved contagious. Pretty soon it was kicking off all over Germany. In March, the Prussian king consented, under considerable duress, to a written constitution. Revolt in Berlin brought two hundred and forty-seven corpses to the streets. In mid-May, a National Assembly was brought together in Frankfurt. It lasted barely a year. In Dresden things were initially a little more restrained. But the membership of the radical, republican Vaterlandsverein union swelled – among its numbers were Richard Wagner, his assistant conductor August Röckel, and the opera house architect Gottfried Semper.

When a deputation from the Vaterlandsverein petitioned the Saxon king in the immediate aftermath of the French Revolution, one of their principal demands was for a free press. The king refused. But the union, in possession of its own facilities, continued printing its pamphlets and newspapers regardless. The most radical of these publications was the *Volksblätter*, edited by Wagner's assistant Röckel, and for a brief time, in Röckel's absence, by Wagner himself. It is in his speeches and writing from this time that we first catch a glimpse, not only of Wagner the revolutionary, but of Wagner the futurist.

"What do you see around you?" Wagner demanded of his audience during a speech to the Vaterlandsverein in June of 1848, later printed and widely distributed. "Dejection and pitiful poverty; everywhere the horrid pallor of hunger and want." He asks for freedom, universal suffrage, and self-determination, but is explicit in this address that his aim is not "communism," a philosophy he considers doomed. He insists, nonetheless, that if the people's demands are continually ignored, then "the wild cry of victory might be that of communism, and although the impossibility of any lengthened duration of its principles as a ruling power can be boldly predicted, yet even the briefest reign of such a thraldom might be sufficient to expunge for a long time to come all the advantages of a civilization of two thousand years old." As they used to say on *Dragnet*, that's not a threat; it's a promise.

By the following April, his writing had grown even more intense. A poem called 'Revolution' appeared in the *Volksblätter*. It was written in a febrile first-person from the point-of-view of the revolution itself, here personified as some sort of avenging goddess. "Down to its very memory I will destroy every trace of this insane order of things," it promises, at an almost Biblical pitch of apocalyptic hysteria. "So up, you people of the earth! Up, you mourners, you oppressed, you poor!... Up, follow my steps in all your multitude and variety, for no distinction can I make among those who follow me!"

In the short interval separating these two discourses, a

commanding new figure had arrived in Dresden. His influence is clearly felt in the fiery clamour of this latter polemic. "Everything about him was colossal!" Wagner would write of Mikhail Bakunin in his autobiography several decades later, evidently still impressed. The fulsome Russian anarchist had arrived in Saxony in the midst of some sort of grand tour of European civil unrest, stopping off at barricades across Germany and beyond. Somehow he succeeded in drawing the composer under his wing. The language of Wagner's 'Revolution' text could almost have been written off Bakunin's own prompt cards.

"The annihilation of all civilisation was the objective on which he had set his heart," wrote Wagner in his autobiography. Bakunin, he said, "offered the consolatory thought that the builders of the new world would turn up of their own accord; we, on the other hand, would have to worry only about where to find the power to destroy. Was any of us insane enough to believe he would survive after the goal of annihilation had been reached? It was necessary, he said, to picture the whole European world, with Petersburg, Paris, and London, transformed into a pile of rubble: how could we expect the arsonists themselves to survey these ruins with the faculty of reason intact?"

Bakunin was far from alone in dreaming of ruins. To the romantic century, the ruin had begun as a source of the picturesque, of serene contemplation. On his grand tour of Italy, the painter Louis Ducros had rendered the crumbling remains of classical civilisation as a glorious edifying spectacle, a window looking out onto some lost golden age. For Walter Scott, in a novel like *Kenilworth*, a ruined castle could be a portal into vivid reveries about the past.

But a nascent literary trend was starting to see the ruin as a place of potential, the site of a possible rebirth. Joseph Méry's tale 'Les ruines de Paris' had sent two travellers from the Atlasian phalanstery of the thirty-sixth century back to visit the rubble of old France. Alfred Franklin's later 'Les ruines de Paris en 4875' saw a military attachment arriving from the French people's new base of Caledonia to find their former capital in a "wretched" state. Following imperial orders, having cleared away what was left of the old Paris, they set about building anew—only to fall prey to certain indigenous insurrectionary spirits, still haunting the ruins.

Wagner was captivated by such images. He set about drafting

the plan for a new libretto whose subject would be nothing less than the death of the gods, the end of a world governed by alien sovereignty in an epic conflagration, and the beginning of a new world of human self-determination. Imagining the work as a direct incitement to revolution, the twilight of the gods as the funeral pyre of social relations, he dreamt of performing it in a specially built theatre on the banks of the Rhine and burning it down after this sole performance. It would be close to three decades before the mammoth four-opera cycle *Der Ring des Nibelungen* finally received its full premiere. When it did, Wagner's new theatre at Bayreuth would be a union of far more than just "all the arts." It would corral a highly sophisticated technological machinery to work directly upon the senses of its audience, combining the proto-cinematic visual projections of the magic lantern with an array of psychoacoustic effects and illusions into what Friedrich Kittler would recognise as "the first mass-medium in the modern sense of the word." By that time, a little of *The Ring*'s chiliastic fervour had cooled off (not that much). But it remains one of the many ironies of Wagner's story that a work intended as a bonfire for all idols and icons would itself end up the object of cult-like worship.

When the time came, and the Saxon king called in Prussian troops against his own people, Wagner was in the very thick of the action. On the third of May 1849, he wrote an editorial in *Die Völksblatter* describing "the appearance of the crowds streaming through our streets," whose presence "made clear enough that what everybody undoubtedly wanted was going to happen." The very next day, his prophecy came true. Barricades were formed and fighting broke out in the streets. Shots were fired. Wagner filled hand grenades, printed and distributed pamphlets, passed messages, kept watch. Wilhelmine Schröder-Devrient, the lead soprano of Wagner's opera house, the Venus in his production of *Tannhäuser*, was heard screaming "*Rächt euch an der Reaktion!*" ("Revenge yourselves upon the reactionaries!") upon seeing from her second-floor window the dead body of a local miner, shot by royalist troops. Her cry spurred on the street fighters.

It is difficult to escape the impression from accounts of the Dresden revolt, of the whole siege as itself a kind of grand opera, with its prima donna, its clashing spear carriers and chorus members following orders communicated by a pair of orchestral conductors from the court theatre. Even the barricades that lined the streets, posing unique problems to a military then unaccustomed to urban warfare, were in large part the work of Gottfried Semper, the architect and set-designer of the opera house. Dresden had become a stage upon which history performed itself as *dramma eroicomico*. When it all ended in tragedy, Wagner would escape only by a fluke, earning his place on a Wanted poster as he flew.

It was in exile that Wagner's career as a polemicist really took off. Living in Zurich, cut off from music and exiled from Germany, he turned to prose. In particular he would find inspiration from a writer introduced to him by Bakunin before the revolution. Ludwig Feuerbach had published his *Principles of the Philosophy of the Future* in 1843. Its pledge was to lead philosophy "out of the realm of departed spirits back to the realm of embodied, living spirits." If Feuerbach's hope had been for a philosophy that would take the place of religion, fulfilling its vital function and thus displacing the need people seemed to have for it, this was largely what Wagner hoped for the operas he was now planning. As he set down his own artistic philosophy, he chose a title as close as possible to Feuerbach's and inscribed a dedication to him on its title page. The whole book is no more, Wagner claims, than the attempt of one artist to interpret Feuerbach's thought for the benefit of other artists, "and indeed to no-one else."

The Artwork of the Future traces the evolution of each separate form of art – poetry, drama, music, sculpture, architecture, and dance – towards a peak at which it strains at its own limits and reaches out towards some unifying grand synthesis to come. His favoured example was the sudden appearance of a choir intoning the words of Friedrich Schiller in the final movement of Beethoven's Ninth symphony. In this moment, Wagner believed, the art of tone reaches beyond itself "into the realm of universal Art."

Wagner's notion of a *Gesamtkunstwerk* was to unite "every branch of Art into the common artwork...in it each separate branch of art is at hand in its own utmost fullness...for the purpose of each separate branch of art can only be fully attained by the reciprocal agreement and co-operation of all the branches in their common message." The narrative recalls the mythic origin story employed by the Florentine Camerata, here repeated and reversed. Where Galilei and his fellows projected a spurious union of the arts into the past, Wagner emphasised its fulfilment in the future. Only through the process of producing such a work could the new "manhood of the future" arise as a "free artistic fellowship," united by the common purpose of an artwork inseparable from life itself whose author would be the collective will of the people. Through association comes freedom. This was the rhetoric of the Dresden revolt, applied to the sphere of opera.

2.7 The Age of Criticism

Das Kunstwerk der Zukunft was published in Leipzig at the end of 1849, barely six months after Wagner's flight from Dresden. At that time, and for several years afterwards, no-one would touch Wagner's operas – except Liszt. To every other theatre in Europe, they were as good as poison. But Liszt's shepherding of *Lohengrin* onto the Weimar stage in 1850, followed by a steady stream of puff-pieces in the *Neue Zeitschrift* in the succeeding years, finally began to pique the interest of curious onlookers.

No less than thirty-six articles in Brendel's paper bore Wagner's name, either as author or subject, between 1850 and the end of 1852. That, as Wagner would later recall, was the year the "hailstorm" began. Between 1852 and 1853 his operas were either being performed or planned for performance in Leipzig, Frankfurt, Wiesbaden, Würzburg, Breslau, Düsseldorf, Rudolstadt, Hamburg, and Riga. The small town of Schwerin managed fourteen performances of *Tannhäuser* in 1852 alone (if only each of those theatres had paid the composer a proper royalty instead of the measly one-off "honorarium" that was then customary, the appalling financial situation that plagued his years of exile might have all been sorted out). But Wagner himself, still a wanted man, could attend none of them. Cut off from his music, he continued to write – and his writing grew evermore strident.

In the tenth of July 1852 edition of *Dwight's Journal of Music*, there ran an article under the headline 'Literary Musicians'. "The present is evidently the age of criticism," it began. "The artists themselves are critics. Once the musician lived in his world of music... But to-day the musician is a creature of to-day: he has a theory of his art, he criticises his world even in the performance, he finds his way into the newspapers, he journalises, he analyses his compeers, he speculates about the music of the Future, and by words as well as deeds would fain herald some new Era in Art." By way of example, it cites four names, considered by the author "perhaps the greatest in the field of actual musical creation": Robert Schumann, Hector Berlioz, Franz Liszt, and Richard Wagner.

Over the preceding years all four of these composers had published an extensive catalogue of writing, chiefly – though not exclusively – about music. Schumann had created the *Neue Zeitschrift für Musik* in 1834 and remained its editor-in-chief for ten years, writing over a thousand pages of criticism in a highflown, picturesque style often taking the form of a dialogue between two fictional characters called Florestan and Eusebius, representing different aspects of his own personality. Liszt's essays, in particular those concerning Wagner's music, were equally poetic, and decidedly novel for their time, drawing from their musical sources a series of vividly described visual images as if they were pages in a picture book.

Berlioz had led perhaps the most illustrious writing career. Ever since landing the job of music critic to the *Journal des Débats* in 1834, he had become one of the most powerful critics in France. For some forty years it was his principal source of income. But by far his strangest written work was for Maurice Schlesinger's *Revue et gazette musicale*. It took the form of neither concert review nor essay, but a series of letters – from the year 2344.

Through these letters, ostensibly between two friends named Xilef and Rotceh, readers were introduced to a futuristic utopia: a city named Euphonia which "can be looked upon as a vast conservatory of music, since the exercise of this art is the sole purpose of its inhabitants' labours." Every Euphonian citizen is engaged permanently with music, be it composing, performing, manufacturing instruments, or research into the science of acoustics. The very structure of the town's districts and streets is arranged like an orchestra, divided by instruments and instrumental section.

But if Berlioz's future fiction sounds far-fetched – it does, after all, end with the death of nineteen people, crushed inside a contracting steel pavilion whose vice-like clench is triggered by the playing of an imaginary hybrid instrument called the "orchestra-piano" – it nonetheless resonates curiously with another text by the same author, published in the same year. In his *Grand traité d'instrumentation et d'orchestration modernes*, Berlioz presents a schema for orchestral deployment every bit as visionary as that in his short science-fiction story. He promoted strange new instruments (some now familiar, like the saxophone and concertina, others, like the octobass, less so), electrical devices to aid conductors, and spoke of an "electric glow" between a conductor and their musicians, as if telegraph wires ran from the one's baton to the other's eyes. Instruments and their players became fused, in Berlioz's imagination, into strange cyborg assemblages: "machines endowed with intelligence." He even had this scheme for combining at once all the instrumental forces available in Paris. He pictures this hypothetical band of eight hundred and twenty-seven players, parsing it carefully into the perfect division and combination of forces. It is as though the map of Euphonia were being transposed to the French capital, as an urge to the city's rebuilding as itself a vast conservatory of music. You can see why it might appeal to *Dwight's Journal*.

Dwight's was a rather unique sort of journal, run by a fairly unique man. John Sullivan Dwight had been director of the school at Brook Farm, an experimental Massachusetts commune inspired by the writings of Charles Fourier. Whilst there, he had taken charge of the musical life of the phalanstery, giving instrumental lessons, organising concerts, and writing on music for the Farm's own newspaper, *The Harbinger*. For several years, Dwight struggled to make Brook Farm the exception amongst American Fourierist groups in acceding (to a degree) to Fourier's own emphasis on music. There was an accomplished "social choir", an active music publishing press, and at one point even an open air opera theatre nestled in a pine grove.

When the experiment went bust in 1847, Dwight moved to Boston and tried to make a living as a music journalist, finally starting his own journal– *Dwight's*–in 1852. Though he never made it to Europe himself until 1860, he was particularly enthusiastic about German culture, a passion that was nurtured by the arrival in Boston of one Otto Dresel, a former piano student of Liszt's who had fled Germany in 1848 after his own involvement in the failed revolutions. Dresel turned up in Boston and befriended Dwight at the beginning of July 1852, just a few days before the paper published its piece on 'Literary Musicians'. Together, they would become amongst the most respected and influential music critics in nineteenth-century America.

But what's interesting about 'Literary Musicians' is that it is not just an article about a group of forward-looking musicians. It is almost a kind of *mise-en-abyme*: a critical text identifying a trend amongst the era's most progressive composers to write and publish their own critical texts. It's as if in order to fundamentally change the nature of music – and change it these four composers certainly did, from a moment's listening you can hear whether a piece was composed before or after them – it was necessary to engage in a thorough reflection on the music of the present and the past, in and through the most important mass media of the day: publishing. The publishing industry was transforming the economic basis of music. And through publishing, Schumann, Berlioz, Liszt, and Wagner would demonstrate and propagandise for a new aesthetics of sound.

Six months after the article in *Dwight's*, the *Rheinische Musik-Zeitung*, edited by Ludwig Bischoff, would identify Wagner as the "representative of the music of the future," accusing him of "whimsical novelty-seeking" and "voice-ruining" music. Probably this is what got Wagner's goat. After all, as Brendel would patiently attempt to spell out a few years later, Wagner's *Artwork of the Future* had been intended as "a synthesis of the arts … Therefore by speaking of '*Zukunftsmusik*' we single out one art – music – as a separate art, in contradiction to the whole initial intent."

No such protestations were going to stop the London *Musical World* in 1855 from grumbling about the "violences," "noise," and "incoherences," of "the music of the future." Nor Charles Dickens's weekly journal *All The Year Round* complaining that Wagner's power derived purely from "noise and stir," comparing his music to a concert of "broken crockery." *Punch* magazine ran a story under the headline 'The Music of the Future' in which they quipped about tuning all the railway whistles to a specific series of pitches for the sake of "giving the Engineers, the Drivers, and Firemen a musical education."

When Wagner came to Paris to conduct his *Tannhäuser*, the operetta composer Jacques Offenbach even mounted a skit poking fun at this *Musicien de l'avenir*. The scene opened in the Elysian Fields with the great composers, Gluck, Mozart, Grétry, and Weber, awaiting the start of a concert. A man entered, declaring himself the "Composer of the Future," denouncing all music of the past and proclaiming a revolution: There will be no more harmony, no more pitch, no more notes, scales, sharps, or flats!

"No more music then?" enquired Gluck.

"Yes; but a strange, unknown, vague, indescribable music!"

At which, this Composer of the Future commenced his *Symphonie de l'avenir*, only for the *maestri* of the past, scandalised by what they heard, to hound him off the stage.

Hector Berlioz, fearing no doubt that his popular association with Liszt's circle in Weimar would come back to bite him, felt compelled to respond. Within a few days of Offenbach's revue at the Bouffes-Parisiens, he had set out his position in a scabrous review of a series of Wagner-conducted symphonic concerts. "If futurism," he wrote, "means to say that one must contradict what the rules teach us; that we are weary of melody...that the ear is to be scorned...that the witches in *Macbeth* were right: that fair is foul and foul is fair – if that is the religion, and a new one at that, then I am far from confessing it. I never have, am not about to, and never will. I raise my hand and swear: *Non credo!*"

Wagner glowered. In an open letter, brimming with "dear friend"s and flattering words for its addressee, he responded to Berlioz's comments in the French press. Where Berlioz had referred to Wagner's "system," to the "musical code" of his "school," Wagner claimed ignorance of any such "school" or any such "theses." Still he found himself persistently haunted by what he would refer to as "the spectral 'Music of the Future' which plays its so popular pranks." This phantom theory, bearing scant relation to anything he had actually written, would precede Wagner's music wherever it went, transforming, in advance, the way people heard it.

But to what extent was it all justified? Wagner himself wanted none of it. Though he was accused again and again of scorning all harmony, in the early twentieth century, Arnold Schoenberg and his pupils would search in vain for unresolved dissonances in Wagner's scores. "You old fraud!" Hanns Eisler would cry, wagging his finger at this ghost whose famed noise and violence seemed simply to evanesce under scrutiny.

In 2013, I interviewed the American composer Philip Corner. He had been similarly stupefied by a close examination of Wagner's music. For many years, Corner worked on a series of pieces each bearing a title suffixed with, '... as a revelation'. It started with a concert in 1969 in which he took just six bars of Mozart's Piano Concerto in C minor, slowed them right down and played them over and over again, subtly shifting the accents and voicings to bring out material implied or buried within the harmonic structure. The series continued with 'The D Major Chord of the Chopin Prelude as a revelation', and 'Satie's Rose-Cross as a revelation'.

Finally, he began a study of the famously dissonant "Tristan chord" from the overture of Wagner's *Tristan und Isolde*. "For a century and a half they've been saying, this chord – it's fantastic, it doesn't resolve!" he said to me, "but it *does* resolve! I mean, it's a great chord and it's a great opening for the opera, but it's totally clear what key it's in, its functional relationship. It's just *not all that far out*. Oh, the Tristan chord! Nobody knows what it is!" He was laughing by now as he said this to me, still somewhat dumbfounded at having all the years of mystification stripped from this music by the simple act of reading the score and playing it. "It opened the gate to the twentieth century! To atonal music! It's *bullshit!*"

But in a sense, the musicologists that Corner derides were right. Such a fear had been stoked up by Wagner's music – of some phantom "future" music, aught but noise and discord – that it had inadvertently produced a desire for just that. Not only Schoenberg, who as a young man in the 1890s had been an "ardent Wagnerian," but practically everyone we might associate with the genesis of a real music of noises in the early to mid-twentieth century had been through the seemingly obligatory rite of passage through Wagner's music. Pioneers of electronic sounds, tone clusters, and works for percussion alone like Stockhausen, Henry Cowell, and Edgard Varèse repeatedly sung his praises in their youth. Luigi Russolos Futurist manifesto *The Art of Noises* spoke of how Wagner had once "deliciously shaken our hearts" even if, Russolo claimed, he had later grown "fed up" with him. Likewise, Balila Pratella's first 'Manifesto of Futurist Musicians' had praised "the sublime genius of Richard Wagner" and the young F. T. Marinetti had confessed that Wagner stirred up "the delirious heat in my blood and is such a friend of my nerves that willingly, out of love, I would lay myself down with him on a bed of clouds." Then a decade and a half later he demands that we all "leave the corpse of Wagner...in the bestial lust of his devotees." It was, he now insisted, "time to move on!"

Like children led to play with matches, it is as though they were all drawn to Wagner by precisely that which they had been warned was wrong with it. Then, like Philip Corner, having digested it and found it wanting in the very subversive element that its detractors had led them to crave, they moved on, happy to openly declare all those things that Wagner spent half his career forced to disavow. So for the Schoenberg of *Pierrot Lunaire* there truly is no more harmony. For the Varèse of *Ionisation* there is no more pitch. For the Russolo of *Risveglia di una Citta* there are no more notes, scales, sharps, or flats.

It was not so much Wagner himself – the *real* Wagner – or any music he actually committed to manuscript that opened the door to the twentieth century, but rather this *other*, imagined Wagner, the fictional Wagner invented by his enemies. And this is why Offenbach's *Symphonie de l'avenir* is such an interesting piece of music. With its grating discords, its droning longueurs, its sudden bursts of noise and clash of juxtaposed elements, it seems to bear in miniature the whole century of avant-garde composition that followed it.

2.8 Odorchord

In the year Wagner first arrived at Bayreuth train station and determined to make his home there, a young Silesian author named Kurd Lasswitz published his first short story. 'Bis zum Nullpunkt des Seins' opens on a summer's day in 2371, picturing the young Aromasia Ozodes playing a fragrant fantasia on her Odorchord. Invented, Lasswitz informs us, by an Italian named Odorato in 2094, the Odorchord is a keyboard of smells. "Pressure on a key opened the corresponding odorometer and a sophisticated mechanism dampened, spread, or blended the odours."

The scene recalls another tale by the same author, from much later in his career. *Auf Zwei Planeten*, published in 1897, would secure Lasswitz's position as the "father of German science fiction." The young Wernher von Braun, inventor of the V2 rocket and NASA's Saturn V, was a particular fan. "I shall never forget," he wrote in an epigraph to the English edition, "how I devoured this novel with curiosity and excitement as a young man." The plot details the fallout from the discovery at the North Pole of a Martian base and the relationships – sometimes cordial, sometimes not – that develop between the people of Earth and Mars.

At one point a party of German explorers head to Mars themselves. While there, one of them is fortunate enough to experience a Martian work of art. "They found themselves in a large hall, in which one saw nothing but innumerable boxes of different sizes. Inscriptions described the artist and the content of the tactile work of art which they contained. In front of some of the boxes, visitors were sitting in silent meditation, they had put their arms up to the elbows into two openings of the boxes." Isma Torm, the visitor from Earth, is none too impressed. "I cannot feel anything but an alternation between pressing, pulling, tingling, rubbing, pushing," she complains, "– for me it's only a kind of massage."

Between these two scenes – a museum of tactile art and a concert of odours – we get a sense of Lasswitz gnawing at an idea, teasing out its implications and extrapolating from them. But what was he extrapolating from? The obvious answer, reached by William B. Fischer, professor in the Department of World Languages and Literature at Portland State University, is the Wagnerian total work of art. A "not entirely complimentary allusion" at that, notes Fischer in his study of early German science fiction.

Lasswitz was born to a middle class family in Breslau, Silesia (now Wrocław, Poland). His upbringing coincided with the period of Wagner's greatest notoriety. During the author's teenage years, the Breslau opera house had performed almost all of Wagner's operas – *Tannhäuser, Rienzi, Lohengrin,* and *Tristan.* Even if he didn't go to a single one, they would certainly have been written about in the local press and talked about a great deal – especially in a liberal, politically-engaged household such as that maintained by Lasswitz's father. Wagner was a real celebrity, and a controversial one to boot. There were probably jokes. It sounds like a joke: if the artwork of the future is a feast for all the senses, will we all be playing smell organs by 2371?

Nor was Lasswitz the only SF author to feel inspired (or, at least, goaded) by the ideas associated with Wagner and his circle. In

1863 Jules Verne submitted a manuscript to his publisher entitled *Paris in the Twentieth Century*. Set a century after its composition, the story concerned a young man named Michel Dufrénoy. A man out of time, lover of literature in an age of technopoly, Verne's narrative follows Dufrénoy's struggles to find love and gainful employment in a dystopian future France. In one memorable scene, the protagonist's friend Quinsonnas describes to him the contemporary music of the 1960s by requesting that he park his bottom on the keys of a piano. "You've just created modern harmony!" Quinsonnas exclaims.

He goes on to clarify for his astonished friend, "in the last century, a certain Richard Wagner, a sort of Messiah who has been insufficiently crucified, invented the Music of the Future, and we're still enduring it; in his day, melody was already being suppressed, and he decided it was appropriate to get rid of harmony as well." As a consequence, the citizens of this Paris of the future have evolved far larger ears than any previous people. "We are living in an age of wizened tympanums and distorted hearing," says Quinsonnas. "You realise that no one keeps a century of Verdi or Wagner in his ears without that organ having to pay for it." Verne's novel was ultimately rejected by his publisher and it sat in a safe until long after the age in which it was set. It is indicative nonetheless of the attitude of some segments of Parisian society towards Wagner's music and ideas.

But Wagner's contemporary reception was far from all negative. His fans may have been few in number at first but they would prove to be disproportionately influential. Charles Baudelaire attended the same Paris concerts as Berlioz in 1860, but his reaction was quite different. Listening to Wagner conduct orchestral extracts from his operas, the author of *Les Fleurs du mal* felt "something new that I was powerless to define."

Baudelaire's enthusiasm would set the scene for a burgeoning Wagner-mania amongst late nineteenth-century French poets, culminating in the short-lived journal *La revue wagnérienne* (which reprinted an extract of Baudelaire's review in its issue of July 1885). But the Wagner that Baudelaire saw in Paris and subsequently wrote about was a conductor of orchestral excerpts. The poet never saw one of his operas and seemed to have little interest in doing so. It was in the music alone that he found a model for the renewal of his poetry. In this sense, as the French philosopher

Philippe Lacoue-Labarthe has pointed out, Baudelaire's Wagner, the Wagner he bequeathed to a generation of French poets, "is not Wagner."

Founded by Edouard Dujardin, the *revue wagnérienne* lasted barely three years, but it counted amongst its contributors such figures as Paul Verlaine, Jean Richepin, and Stéphane Mallarmé. Within its pages, writers convinced that they were building the new poetic art of the future strove to draft such Wagnerian tropes as the "leitmotif" or "endless melody" into the service of poetry. Unfortunately they had little understanding of what these terms had referred to even in a musical context. There were varying degrees of success.

Nevertheless, the associative, quasi-random "stream-of-consciousness" technique, first pioneered by Dujardin in his works from this period in a specific attempt to recreate in verse the endless melody ascribed to Wagnerian music dramas, would find its adherents across the Channel. James Joyce confessed to having "picked up a copy" of Dujardin's 1888 novel *Les Louriers sont coupées* from a train-station bookseller while visiting Paris in 1903. It must have been well-thumbed by the time he started work on *Ulysses* a decade later.

In the late 1860s, a small group of bourgeois Englishmen and German ex-pats began to meet regularly in each other's London homes to discuss and perform piano reductions of music by Wagner, Liszt, Beethoven, and Berlioz. They initially gave themselves the improbable title of the Working Men's Society, though for the most part their employment came from the music industry (or, in the case of Fritz Hartvigson, from the Prince of Wales). One of their number, a piano student of Liszt's named Walter Bache, gave a recital each April dedicated to the "music of the future" which was greeted annually with a sort of respectful bewilderment by the *Musical Times*. It was called "interesting" and he would be praised more for the sacrifice of giving it a go than any aspect of the performance itself.

But in 1873, another "working man," the Royal College of Music professor Edward Dannreuther, formed the first British Wagner Society with the Earl of Crawford and Balcarres. Together they arranged concerts, propagandised on behalf of the composer, and raised money for Wagner's Bayreuth theatre. Their secretary was one Francis Hueffer, who in 1874 published a book, *Richard*

Wagner and the Music of the Future, and three years later became music editor of *The Times* after his predecessor was edged out by the management for failing to keep up with contemporary tastes.

That, by 1877 – the year Hueffer took over at *The Times* and Wagner himself came to London to conduct six concerts at the Albert Hall – the taste of the "general public" had swung so much in the composer's favour that even previously hostile critics were turning proselytes, was at least in part thanks to the efforts at elucidation of Hueffer himself. His book, however, is notable for claiming on Wagner's behalf a theory of "poetic music" that is nowhere to be found in the composer's own writings. What it does, however, revive is the view from *Dwight's Journal* of thirty years earlier: that Wagner, with Schumann, Liszt, and Berlioz, represented a futurist avant-garde precisely insofar as they were also writers, critics, and "literary musicians."

The attitude of the critic from *Punch* magazine who "went [to Wagner's London concerts] to scoff [but] remained to praise" was typical. And not just in London. In Austria, a parody of Wagner's *Tannhäuser* had been produced by the great Viennese comic Johann Nestroy in 1853. In Nestroy's version, which sounds rather like an early Woody Allen film, the goddess Venus runs an underground delicatessen which the knight, Tannhäuser, flees in order to sing tenor in an opera house "of the future." The music by the now-forgotten composer Carl Binder takes Wagner's riffs and puts them into waltz time, punctuated with the characteristic *whoops* and *tra-la-las* of bar-room *Volkslieder*. At one point the whole thing descends into a mash-up with Mozart and Weber when Tannhäuser sings a *Zukunfts-Zauberflöte* with the lyrics from Weber's *Der Freischütz*. When Wagner's original finally rolled into town a few years later, the out-of-town singers were quite bewildered by the audience's persistent laughter.

Pretty soon other composers were keen to get in on the act. Franz von Suppé, an author of operettas whose music will today be recognisable only to Bugs Bunny fans, produced parodies of both *Tannhäuser* and, with Nestroy again, *Lohengrin* (as *Lohengelb*).

It was not always clear, however, what was intended as satire and what was sincere tribute. An 1859 review of the dress rehearsal for the operetta *Prinz Methusalem* suggested that its composer, Johann Strauss Jr., had included a parody of the theme from *Lohengrin* – only for it to be removed before opening night at the insistence of the Court Opera, which was preparing a production of an actual Wagner opera at the time. But already in 1852, the young Strauss had composed an apparently quite sincere tribute in the form of a medley of tunes from *Lohengrin* performed in concert. The modern harmonies of his *Die Extravaganten* waltz of 1858 bore the distinct influence of this engagement. Johann's brother, Josef, likewise had performed excerpts from *Tristan und Isolde* and *Rienzi*, and the atmospheric introduction of his *Sphären-klänge* has been compared by recent scholars, like Derek Scott, to a Lisztian symphonic poem.

Nor does their enthusiasm seem to have waned. Much later in the century Johann Strauss Jr.'s opera *Ritter Pázmán* was modelled so closely on the Wagnerian *Gesamtkunstwerk* that only Brendel's *Neue Zeitschrift* could stomach it. A reviewer from the *Wiener Allgemeine Zeitung* claimed that Strauss must have been "haunted" by Eva, the female lead from Wagner's *Meistersinger*, when giving his own leading lady the same name in *Ritter Pázmán*. (The influence, incidentally, may not have been all one way. Wagner had recorded in his autobiography experiencing the "frenzy" of Strauss Sr.'s playing when he visited Vienna as a teenager, and it has been claimed – likewise, by Scott – that the music of the flower-maidens scene in *Parsifal* bears more than a whiff of Strauss Jr.'s *Verzückungswalzer*.)

Historians and contemporary observers alike have spoken of the decadence of Viennese society at the end of the nineteenth century. But alongside that, there was also a kind of utopianism. The architect Camillo Sitte first developed his notion of the modern city as a "total work of art" at a meeting of the Wagner Society of Vienna in 1875. He spent the final years of his life planning a vast eight-volume work that would go from the roots of Etruscan building to the great German art of the future.

Artists associated with the new art exhibited at the Secession sought ways of musicalising their prints and paintings. The vision of music they embraced was drawn from the *Zukunftsmusik* ideas associated with Wagner. This culminated in the two Secession exhibitions of 1902 and 1903 featuring Max Klinger's statue of Beethoven and Gustav Klimt's *Beethoven* frieze. Klinger, who would later lay the foundation stone for a Wagner monument in Leipzig, may have chosen Beethoven for his subject in Vienna, but his ambition, as revealed by his diaries, was to reproduce in sculpture "what Wagner strove for and attained in his music dramas." If there were any doubt as to *whose* Beethoven Klimt was representing with his frieze, then it should be assuaged by a glance at the inscription he included under the third panel with its depiction of an ideal world to come: "My kingdom is not of this world," wrote Klimt, quoting the same Biblical passage Wagner had used in his 'Beethoven' essay of 1870.

By the turn of the twentieth century, Wagner's music, as Thomas Mann put it, had "exercised an instructive and nourishing influence on every form of artistic endeavour." But almost all of that influence would be based on a misunderstanding that Wagner himself had spent half his career struggling to correct. Baudelaire, Klimt, and Dujardin had not sought some overarching synthesis, the dissolution of their own discipline into a *Gesamtkunstwerk* of all the arts together. What they aspired to was rather the raising up of their own genre to attain something of the vaunted status of the "music of the future". In painting, sculpture, poetry, architecture, and beyond, artists would look to music as a model, believing they would find in it the herald of some bright tomorrow.

The "music of the future" became a sort of beacon for progressive art in general. And the proper noun attached to that beacon was Wagner's—even if the phrase itself was only ever uttered by the composer in order to scorn it. What had begun as a glib journalistic catchphrase—whether first uttered out of scorn, marketing nous, or simple misunderstanding—finally exerted a profound effect on artistic disciplines far beyond its original sphere of application. Like a virus, this phrase spread throughout the world, creating an indelible association between the art of music and dreams of the future. A mistake, maybe—but a mistake with wings. It is almost certainly what the organisers of the Alpbach forum had in mind, when they invited Ligeti to speak on the subject in 1961. They had in mind, perhaps, a figure like Offenbach's *Musicien de l'avenir*.

2.9 The Meaning of the Message

It is tempting to speculate about how Ligeti's life and music might have been different had he caught that train out of East Berlin in the summer of 1952. Perhaps the tentative year zero announced by the "static, self-contained" piano suite *Musica Ricercata* would have remained in his desk drawer, forever unfinished. On the other hand perhaps it would have made little difference.

But that was not what Ligeti himself concluded. "If I had taken the subway," he later reflected, "I would never have had the chance to be with the Cologne-Darmstadt people because Britain was very much apart... I would have been part of swinging London!" One can only imagine what effect a young and restless György Ligeti, with his enormous compositional talent, his interest in the dense hocketing textures of medieval polyphony, and his thirst for the strange sounds of electronic music, might have had on the pop scene of 1950s England.

Instead, after finally escaping from Budapest to Vienna in 1956, Ligeti was granted a scholarship to study in Cologne at the electronic music studios of the Westdeutscher Rundfunk. Opened in 1951 in the West German radio station's Broadcasting Centre, the Studio für elektronische Musik was one of the world's first workshops for the creation of music by purely electronic means. But its founder was not a composer. He was a linguist.

Werner Meyer-Eppler, of the Phonetics Institute at the University of Bonn, had grown interested in the possibilities for electronic sound production after seeing a demonstration of the Vocoder when visiting Bell Labs in America. He was one of Germany's leading experts on information theory, an abstract mathematical model of communication developed by telephone engineers and cryptographers as a means of simplifying certain problems in their own particular fields. It is thanks to information theory that we have a measure for information itself, in "bits."

In the middle decades of the twentieth century, information theory began to have an effect on domains way beyond its original bailiwick, from economics to evolutionary biology. It possessed a simplicity and a mathematical elegance that was enormously seductive. Its influence on music was vast but is little talked about today. It made possible both Muzak and the mp3. It is referenced in John Cage's *Silence* and the notes to Alvin Lucier's *North American Time Capsule*. Its veneer of scientific objectivity made it a favoured tool of musical analysis. For many composers it provided a way in to thinking about making music with machines, and continued to inform their thinking about music when they returned to instrumental writing.

One of Ligeti's first electronic pieces at the WDR studio was called *Artikulation*, essentially a study in the creation of an artificial spoken syntax, created under the influence of Meyer-Eppler's ideas. *Artikulation* is full of sounds that resemble natural language: there are sudden hard consonants, sentence-like bursts, and sequences of pitches inflected with the distinctive final upturn of enquiry, as if these clusters of sine tones were plaintively asking the listener a question. But it ultimately refers to nothing at all. It talks a lot, but it's not saying anything.

This is precisely in keeping with the way Bell Labs's Claude Shannon had formulated information theory in the first place. "In communication engineering, we are interested in transmitting messages from one point to another," Shannon announced to a meeting of the American Statistical Society, a few days after Christmas in 1949. "The 'meaning' of the message (if any) is irrelevant to the engineering problem." He's right, of course – from an engineering perspective. If your phone lines are down, whoever comes round to fix them does not need to know what you were talking about with your aunt in Worcester at the time. But what happens when the same principles are applied to fields to which people do indeed tend to attach a great deal of meaning – like music?

Around the time Ligeti was learning about information theory in Cologne, an Illinois chemistry professor named Lejaren Hiller was using the same means to program a computer to compose music from scratch. He named his results the *Illiac Suite*, a string quartet named after its composer, the Illinois Automatic Computer (or ILLIAC). The push-button "composing machine," once prophesied by the critic Richard Pohl in Weimar back in the 1850s, was finally coming to life.

'Mechanical Brain Takes Up Composing Music' was the headline in the *Champaign-Urbana News Gazette*. Hiller worked for a little over a year with the University of Illinois's "super programmer" Leonard Isaacson, finally producing a four-movement work for live instrumentalists by November of 1956. Each individual note was generated by the computer using random numbers tested against certain predefined criteria and statistical parameters. The precise method was based on techniques developed at Los Alamos for predicting the dispersal of radioactive neutrons after a nuclear explosion.

To critics who accused them of concocting a parody of music's rich emotional life, Hiller and Isaacson insisted that "Music is a sensible form. It is governed by laws of organization which permit fairly exact codification ... it follows that computer-produced music which is 'meaningful' is conceivable to the extent to which the laws of musical organization are codifiable." The scare quotes here are telling. Meaning itself had to be redefined, rendered computable, "codifiable." As justification they referred to Shannon's information theory.

But they might just as well have cited Eduard Hanslick's "form moving in sound" – or, for that matter, Adam Smith. For even as *The Wealth of Nations* made him an early prophet of free-market capitalism, Smith was refining his old lecture notes on aesthetics, finally published posthumously with the title, 'Of the Nature of that Imitation which takes place in what are called the Imitative Arts'. "Melody and harmony," wrote Smith, "signify and suggest nothing." And even in the case of a piece of music – such as a song, dance, or opera – which *did* seem to have specific meanings attached by the association of another art form, the music itself could act only "like a transparent mantle," which might lend a "more enlivening lustre" to the meanings and sentiments already expressed.

When I was at university, in the first years of the twenty-first century, it was considered practically a given that music could have no intrinsic meanings. A piece of music may be meaningful to you, or to specific social groups, in certain contexts, under certain conditions, but it does not in itself bear meaning. We were taught to think of music "as communication" (as the title of one semester-long course put it). But just as in information theory, the actual significance of whatever was being communicated remained obscure, or irrelevant. To focus on meaning itself was a corruption of the signal.

The situation in academia would appear to have changed little since the 1850s, when Hanslick was encouraged to scrub from his second edition every last trace of the cosmic or referential in favour of a renewed emphasis on "the methods of the natural sciences." The legitimacy of any pursuit derives from its divorce from reality, its aptness to a kind of dry contemplation "not unlike," in Adam Smith's words, "that which derives from the contemplation of a great system in any other science."

Hiller and Isaacson detailed the progress of their composition in the manner of a "laboratory notebook." Each stage was patiently sub-headed – experimental methods, experimental procedures, experimental results, and so on – in precisely the fashion in which Hiller had once written up his chemistry experiments. It was, after all, as a chemist, calculating the constitution of polymer molecules, that he had first come across the procedures he here applied to pitched notes. There was almost no reason for him to see it any differently. They called the book *Experimental Music*, the phrase still very much alive with its associations with the comforting legitimations of the science lab and white coat.

John Cage, in his lectures from the late 1950s, had enthusiastically adopted this term "experimental music". Not, he would insist, "as descriptive of an act to be later judged in terms of success and failure," but instead, "simply as of an act the outcome of which is unknown." The term grew in currency, though for some it remained objectionable. Edgard Varèse, in particular, resented its suggestion of trial and error, as if he were presenting to the public mere research notes. But for Pierre Schaeffer, the adoption of "*musique expérimentale*" signified a turn towards research, "empiricism," a turn towards a consideration of "sonic objects as such." For the German, Wolfgang Rebner, American experimental music was related to America's pioneering scientific spirit. By the time of Michael Nyman's landmark 1974 book, *Experimental Music: Cage and Beyond*, "experimental" had become a term for any music in which "personal expression, drama, psychology, and the like" had become "at best gratuitous", any music, that is, which "obliterates the past, and…removes the possibility of a future."

Only in such a context, this peculiar cloud of misunderstanding and mutual incomprehension, can we begin to grasp why a think tank like the Alpbach European Forum would invite a figure like Ligeti to speak at a conference on 'Science in the Future'. Music itself was posing as a science, with its own formal rules and experimental procedures. But at the same time, it was also the reason why it was impossible for him to say anything, since that very scientism cemented its divorce from reality. Once meaning had necessarily been bracketed out of music, how can anyone speak about the future?

The Alpbach Social Forum was intended to be a pleasant alpine getaway for intellectuals to mull over the future of a new united Europe. It was created in the immediate post-war period, around the same time as other think tanks like the RAND Corporation and Mont Pelerin Society. But gradually the focus of its colloquia shifted from politics to economics. Prominent amongst the guests to Alpbach at this time were a group of Austrian thinkers clustered around the Viennese economist Friedrich Hayek, including Fritz Machlup, Gottfried von Haberler, Karl Popper, and Ludwig von Mises.

In 1947, Hayek had convened a group of intellectuals at another alpine retreat, five hundred kilometres away in the Swiss resort of Mont Pèlerin, among them Machlup, Haberler, Popper, and von Mises. Hayek was convinced that the rise of totalitarian states in Soviet Russia and Nazi Germany were both equally the result of believing that governments could intervene positively in people's lives. Instead, he was convinced that governments should only intervene in order to make it easier for businesses to operate and for finance to flow around the world. Since the markets, in Hayek's view, so perfectly represented and regulated people's desires, it was illogical – even immoral – to do anything to stand in their way.

In 1947, with the Labour Party steadily building a new welfare state in the UK, and socialist or social-democratic parties in power in France, Belgium, and much of Scandinavia, the views of Hayek and his friends were pretty far outside the mainstream of economic thinking for the time. But thanks to the influential positions of certain members of Hayek's Mont Pelerin Society, not to mention the wealth they showered on sponsoring university chairs and think tanks, they would grow increasingly influential over the succeeding years.

Hayek first visited the European Forum in Alpbach during the summer of 1947, mere months after founding the Mont Pelerin Society. Speaking in Alpbach that summer he would argue that what he termed the "order of the economy" should be considered "one of the most important tasks which the human mind can pose itself today." He found Alpbach "charming and stimulating" and started persuading his friends to come on a regular basis. Pretty soon more and more members of his Mont Pelerin Society began taking their summers in the Austrian Alps. By 1961, the year Ligeti arrived in Alpbach, seminars under topics like 'Great Britain and the European Continent Today' were almost entirely eclipsed by the likes of 'Capital Formation and Capital Market' or 'City and Countryside in the Age of Technology'.

Amongst Hayek's friends at the Mont Pelerin Society, one man in particular had his eyes on the future. Bertrand de Jouvenel was a former journalist, who in the mid-Thirties had interviewed Adolf Hitler, rather flatteringly, for the popular magazine *Paris-Midi*. But by the end of the Second World War he was thoroughly disillusioned with politics of all kinds. Like Hayek, he regarded any attempt at the redistribution of wealth as "a transfer of power from individuals to officials." Eventually, however, he would go off to form his own think tank with a substantial grant from the Ford Foundation. It was called *Futuribles*. The name was chosen, he claimed, to avoid the scientific pretensions of "futurology." The future, he insisted in his *The Art of Conjecture*, "is not a domain of objects passively presented to our knowledge." Rather, he saw in his forecasts a leap of the imagination, a creative act reaching forward and building a picture in front of him. "The intellectual construction of a likely future," he said, "is a work of art, in the full sense of the term."

Here is the peculiarity of this moment at the beginning of the Sixties. We have artists pretending they are scientists and bureaucrats fancying themselves artists. The neoliberal coterie around Hayek and de Jouvenel were a fringe movement in the middle years of the twentieth century. But they were building something. They had money and rich backers, and they used their resources to fund more think tanks and several chairs at elite universities. György Ligeti may have had nothing to say about the future that summer day in 1961, but these men had plenty to spare.

Interval: 2015

By nine minutes past ten, the Minguett Quartett had been sawing to and fro through Morton Feldman's second string quartet, like a rusty gate in a gentle breeze, for a little over four hours. As the art critic Amelia Groom had pointed out during a seminar earlier that day, nine past ten is the time watches are always set to in magazine ads, as if frozen in some never-ending cocktail hour. The close harmonies of Feldman's piece, alternately scintillating and severe, seem caught in just such a permanent present. The tempo never changes but time itself seems to speed up, slow down, and finally disappear altogether.

There is an inevitable physical dimension to such durations. One becomes acutely aware of the ill-fit between bum, back, and chair. A parade of small itches is made manifest. You become intimately acquainted with the many small sounds of all your neighbours' bodies. This physicality was emphasised, too, in the Minguett's performance: the tender grain of wood and horsehair strings was ever-present. But through these small sounds, Feldman's writing evokes vast spaces: broad horizons and wide open fields.

I was deep in the belly of a former East German power station for a concert called The Long Now. The doors opened at six p.m. on a Saturday evening and the music went on until midnight on Sunday. But this was no rave or all-night dance party. By the early hours of Sunday morning, the main hall was speckled with fold-out cots, draped with silver and gold emergency blankets, while the walls still shook to the thunderous microtonal drones of Phill Niblock. Named after a proposal to build a clock to keep ticking for ten thousand years, The Long Now still felt less about time, more about duration. It dealt in music that went on, and on, and on.

Built in the early 1960s, Kraftwerk's interior resembles some vast cathedral of exposed concrete at right angles. Upstairs, a door to the side led into the former control room, which played host to a twenty-four-hour sound installation by Leif Inge called '9 Beet Stretch'. Rectangular in shape, the room's two long walls were covered in grey-green plastic, pocked with myriad old knobs and dials, connected by some obscure pictorial language of painted red, green, and black lines to create some enormous Lissitzkyan flow diagram of sensors and control surfaces. Inge's piece is a stretched-out rendition of Beethoven's Ninth Symphony, slowed down until it sounds more like pure digital synthesis than natural orchestral sound. It recalled at once Laurie Spiegel, My Bloody Valentine, Gustav Mahler, Suzanne Ciani, and some magisterial gothic cathedral sinking slowly into the ocean. What had once been arguably the highpoint of romantic tension-and-release, forward-moving structure, becomes a quasi-static block of sound. Participants have described feeling like "a fly trapped in honey."

The day before the gig, I was at a conference across town in Wilmersdorf, part of the same 'Festival for Time': Maerzmusik. The Italian philosopher Antonio Negri was addressing a small audience of two or three dozen people, at least a couple of whom I recognised as well-known German composers. "Marx's understanding of time is of a time that socialises itself," Negri began. "We can make a history of this socialisation of time, of the primacy of time over space."

From the floor, I asked if maybe he could connect some of these ideas about the shifting sands of temporal regimes to changes in our relationship with music. Negri demurred at first, saying, "I doubt I can give a proper answer." But soon enough he ploughed on. "Temporal perception is fundamental to perception of the real," he said. "We can play different distinctions of musical ages according to this." He concluded with a word about Beethoven's relationship to the metronome, suggestive of music's succumbing to the clock-time of capitalism. But, again, he seemed hesitant, shrugging diffidently. "Maybe this is banal..."

Music takes time. To quote the English essayist Basil de Selincourt, "Music is one of the forms of duration; it suspends ordinary time, and offers itself as an ideal substitute and equivalent." When listening, it is apparent that the time we feel can become radically dislocated from the time of the clock. It seems to speed up or slow down, reach forward or hang in suspension. Listening to Morton Feldman in Berlin, it was palpable. As the composer Jonathan Kramer suggests in his book *The Time of Music*, this sensation is key to music's meaningfulness. "Music becomes meaningful," he writes, "in and through time."

Drum your fingers on the table when bored and the rhythm seems to speed the waiting on. Sing a favourite old song to recall happy times past or ward off fears of things to come. In countless similar ways, music has long been used to provide structure to the day, the year, or even longer periods of time: music for harvest time, for remembrance, to augur or forestall. We know Christmas is coming when all the shops start playing Christmas songs. We know *Seinfeld* is about to start on the telly when we hear that slap-bass intro. And who among us doesn't salivate to the sound of George Gershwin's *Rhapsody in Blue*, like one of Ivan Pavlov's obedient puppies, ever since its use in a TV advertisement for Galaxy chocolate bars?

Music is a machine for producing anticipation. Over the course of about three hundred years, from the end of the renaissance to the turn of the twentieth century, the tonal system of Western classical music was gradually engineered to become an extraordinarily sophisticated system for managing that anticipation. Certain chords would seem to beckon other chords to follow them. A sonata theme looked forward eagerly to its own recapitulation. Every note, every phrase would be precisely tailored to set up particular expectations that would either be fulfilled or frustrated, producing specific sensations in the listener.

The harmonic structure of chords and keys managed far more than just how prettily different notes might sit on top of each other. It regulated the structure of a piece on both a macro and micro level in countless ways that some composers and songwriters continue to take advantage of to this day (whether consciously or not).

In a 2007 book called *Bach's Cycle, Mozart's Arrow*, the Polish-American musicologist Karol Berger borrows a distinction from Stephen Jay Gould in order to draw a line between two different images for the passing of time: the circle and the arrow. For Gould, the former implies a world in which, "Fundamental states are immanent in time, always present and never changing. Apparent motions are parts of repeating cycles, and differences in the past will be realities of the future. Time has no direction." On the other hand, the metaphor of "time's arrow" suggests "an irreversible sequence of unrepeatable events" in which "all moments, considered in proper sequence, tell a story of linked events moving in one direction."

Gould presents this dyad as a kind of deep structure in Judaeo-Christian thinking, between the two poles of which Western thought has persistently swung. But for Berger, the shift he perceives in the history of music, from structures shaped cyclically to those directed like arrows, marks a decisive break. It is the beginning of musical modernity. He locates that break in the middle decades of the eighteenth century, roughly contemporary with Louis-Sebastien Mercier's publication of *L'an 2440*.

In a series of detailed analyses of works by Johann Sebastian Bach, Berger shows how the Leipzig kapellmeister repeatedly seeks to "neutralise time" even as the music unfolds "in time." There is a crystalline quality to the typical Bach fugue, such that everything that unfolds is really just a different facet of the same gleaming surface. His oratorios make skilful use of repetition in order to effectively stage the abolition of temporal succession. As the work unfolds, what once was sequential becomes simultaneous; past, present, and future become telescoped into an "eternal Now."

With Mozart, born six years after Bach's death in 1756, everything has changed. Musical form has become temporal and understanding that form requires following the succession of parts through time. To follow a Mozart instrumental concerto is to trace a distinct path towards its goal; a Mozart opera does not return its characters to their starting point, as operas of a century (or even a few decades) earlier tended to. Instead, it leaves the whole situation fundamentally transformed. The valet, Figaro, gets the drop on his master. The closed, feudal world of *The Magic Flute* has transformed, by the final curtain, into an enlightened universal brotherhood. Such transformations – which, in a way, stage the very question of what it means for something to transform, and for history to take place – are reflected as much in the structure of individual passages of music as they are in the overall shape of the narrative. "Time's cycle had been straightened into an arrow," writes Berger, "and the arrow was traveling ever faster."

History itself became an arrow in Mozart's time. To borrow Gould's words, it began to "tell a story of linked events moving in one direction." The historian Reinhart Koselleck relates how the German word *Geschichte* replaced the earlier loan word *Historie*. Where the latter had suggested a simple report of events in succession, the former became a kind of *thing*–history *itself*. It had unity, universality, even a sort of agency. Negri, in Berlin, had spoken of the music of the seventeenth century in these terms, as "a sequence of temporal events" – in effect, as *Historie*, lacking quite the narrative drive or coherence of *Geschichte*. But just as

Negri suggested, time was changing in more ways than one.

There had been clocks in English towns and villages since the fourteenth century. But in an essay called 'Time, Work-Discipline, and Industrial Capitalism', the historian E.P. Thompson suggests that they remained for a long time notoriously unreliable. Many people still tended to rely on sundials to set the time on the clocktower. Accuracy was improved by the pendulum clocks of the late seventeenth century. That and the pocket-watch invented by Christiaan Huygens (whose escapement – that's the bit that controls and makes countable the unfurling of the spring – would later find its way into the design of the first piano) made time more dependable and a little more pervasive amongst certain classes, but clocks remained expensive. "Ornate and rich design," Thompson remarks, "was still preferred to plain serviceability."

All that began to change in the last decades of the eighteenth century, thanks partly to a thriving black market driven by pickpockets. As workers moved to the towns to clock-in for factory shifts, they did so increasingly with a watch on their wrist and a grandfather clock in their parlour. Composers would not escape the swinging of the pendulum. The metronome was invented around 1812. Though today his authorship is disputed, the device was patented by Johann Nepomuk Maelzel, chief engineer to the Viennese court, in 1815. The first metronome markings in beats-per-minute to appear on a printed score can be found in works by Maelzel's close friend, Ludwig van Beethoven, from around this time (Maelzel designed the composer's hearing aid). The rigid, staccato pattern that opens the second movement of the composer's Eighth Symphony is sometimes said to be an affectionate parody of the metronome's regular swing. By the time Liszt and Wagner were in regular correspondence, with the former engaged in presenting the latter's work in his absence, a significant part of those letters would be taken up with bickering over the proper metronome markings.

Over the course of the last century, a great deal of music has been produced that aspires to a state of timelessness. Eschewing the arrow-like thrust of the nineteenth century, composers have returned to the cycles and stasis of a Bach fugue. Olivier Messiaen's Quartet for the End of Time, written in a German prisoner-of-war camp in 1941, is riddled with harmonic changes and rhythmic figures that work the same way forwards and backwards. The score instructs performers in the fifth movement to play "infinitely slow." Stockhausen's "moment-form" pieces, like *Momente* and *Carré*, sought, in the composer's words, "the overcoming of the concept of duration" by leaving the ordering of different passages indeterminate. Morton Feldman spent most of his career trying to erase any sense of metre from his music, using graphic scores with only vaguely determined attack points or deliberately confusing ways of writing rhythms in traditional notation, in order, as he put it, to make time "less perceptible as movement, more conceivable as image."

There is a certain irony in the way recent composers will so consistently present as "radical" temporal forms that for J.S. Bach, four hundred years ago, represented the unchanging dominion of God. For a Catholic composer like Messiaen, this is explicit. His score is inscribed "in homage to the Angel of the Apocalypse." Less so for those who followed him. If we can accept the idea that the time sense expressed in music can somehow model, reflect, or even affect the passing of time in social life, then it should be obvious that any music which implies unchanging persistence – or, for that matter, change so slight, so gradual, so subtle that you could be forgiven for not noticing it – can hardly count as radical. For the greater part of a century, we have been stuck in Messiaen's end of time, as if the "infinitely slow" fifth movement of his *Quartet* had been taken at his word, and was still going on.

In fact, it's probably only a matter of time until someone really does take him at his word. There are enough projects going on already that take a lead from Messiaen's hyperbolic tempo marking. Since the fifth of September 2001, a performance of John Cage's 1987 piece *Organ2/ASL (As SLow aS Possible)* has been ongoing at St. Buchardi church in Halberstadt, Germany. Kicking off with a seventeen-month pause, and with several years separating some of the chord changes, the work is scheduled to conclude in September 2640, six hundred and thirty-nine years after it began. Even more extreme is the work *Longplayer* by Jem Finer, formerly the banjo player in The Pogues, which sounded its first notes on the first day of the year 2000 (in London's Millennium Dome, no less) and, barring any unforeseen circumstances, will continue until the end of the millennium, sounding its final cadence on the thirty-first of December, 2999.

Of course, the absence of unforeseen circumstances is precisely what both of these enterprises rely on. The *Financial Times* welcomed Finer's work with the headline 'Coming Soon: The Future', but ultimately *Longplayer* relies on a never-ending present to achieve its aims. This prescription is perhaps most explicit in an even more protracted undertaking. Funded by Amazon CEO Jeff Bezos and conceived by computer scientist and Walt Disney imagineer-in-chief Danny Hills, the 'Clock of the Long Now' is supposed to tick once a year, advance its "century hand" every hundred years, and keep time for a good ten thousand years. Brian Eno has been working on the clock's once-a-millennium chimes. Drawing on the seventeenth-century church practice of ringing the changes, Eno has proposed a ten-bell peal, gradually working its way through all 3,628,800 combinations of the ten different notes. If you want a vision of the future, imagine a bell ringing the same ten pitches – forever.

But the new timelessness of the twentieth century was not necessarily opposed to the rules of the clock. The later works of Feldman, in particular, are notable for an extraordinary finickiness with regard to timing. Even John Cage, whilst pledging to let sounds be themselves, continued to prescribe carefully their chronometric position. Take his *4'33"* – everything here is free, *except* the precise length of the three movements, which is specified with greater precision than in almost any piece of music before it, not in beats and bars but the seconds of clock time.

Dutch composer Louis Andriessen's *De Tijd* sought to enact the overcoming of clock time, represented by chiming pitched percussion, with a languorous succession of circulating chords for voice, strings, and organ. He wanted to suggest "a situation of sustained, glorified musical motionlessness." La Monte Young's *Dream House* shifted his practice from drones stretched through time, to tones spread out across a layout in space to be moved through freely by the audience. More recently, Bryn Harrison has worked with not-quite-symmetrical overlapping cycles and complexes of sound like objects viewed in space. His aim is to create musical structures that are "essentially non-goal-related."

In a recent piece for the Issue Project Room in New York, the electronic music producer Mark Fell sought explicitly to critique such dreams of musical timelessness. He presented an extended mix of drone-based, ambient works (including Young and Terry Riley alongside more abrasive material by the Hafler Trio and The Anti-Group). But instead of standing on the stage himself, he placed, in the position traditionally reserved for the performing artist, a very large LED clock set to the correct time "incessantly reminding the audience of exactly how much time they had spent," in order to undermine any possible discourse of atemporal abstraction.

Andriessen dramatises the overcoming of clock time by everlasting timelessness; Fell reverses the equation, emphasising the clock as a means of puncturing the myth of atemporality. But neither grasp a time that would be essentially musical. If the composers of the twentieth century – and Leif Inge's '9 Beet Stretch' – have shown anything, it is that the rigidity of the clock and the timelessness of heaven are not necessarily opposed; more like two sides of the same coin. Perhaps the question of the future of music has become an impossible one for musicians to answer because the music itself is structured in a way that precludes any thought of time really passing and progressing. Music now occupies time only in order to freeze it. It could do so much more.

Third Act: 2079

3.1 Like Water

Gary Sinise is in the shower. It is some sort of futuristic shower, more like a curved wall pockmarked with myriad little jets spraying water at Gary Sinise as he stretches out his right arm and looks down thoughtfully.

"A little hotter," he says. The shower responds to his command. We see the reading on a small domed temperature dial go up by a few degrees. Steam rises. "That's good," says Gary Sinise.

"Music on," he says. A beat kicks in immediately. Snare drums syncopated against hi-hats playing sixteen beats to the bar. A synthesizer billows soft arpeggios in a minor key. The track is called 'Tribal Flight 1' and is taken from a Bruton Music library album called *Future Dance*, produced by composer Richard Downing in 1997. "No, no!" says Gary Sinise irritably. "Something else."

The beat stops. "Hooker," says Gary Sinise, "John Lee." Instantly we recognise the guitar lick that opens John Lee Hooker's 1962 hit record 'Boom Boom'. Gary Sinise is happy. "That's good," he says again. He laughs out loud to himself at nothing in particular as he proceeds to wash himself, accompanied by the Mississippi-born singer's throaty delivery.

This is the year 2079, as envisioned by the 2001 Gary Fleder film, *Impostor*. Music from anywhere, any time, on demand. With a few simple spoken commands, you can conjure up whatever sound you like – whether it's a grumpy old blues song from the early 1960s or some ageing library composer's idea of the future of dance music, from 1997. It's as easy as turning a tap. Easier even.

"Music," said David Bowie in a *New York Times* interview from June 2002, just six months after the release of *Impostor*, "is going to become like running water or electricity." The *Times* was interviewing Bowie at a studio in Manhattan, just a few days before the release of *Heathen*, his twenty-second studio album. The article says very little about his new songs or his impending tour. This is both "one of rock's most astute conceptualists" and "smartest entrepreneurs." In the preceding few years, the singer had created his own technology company (Ultrastar) and internet service provider (Bowienet). Almost uniquely amongst his peers, Bowie had been paying very close attention to developments in communications technology, long before their impact was felt upon his royalty cheques.

The mp3 codec had been released in 1993 by the German Fraunhofer Institute. Using new forms of data compression, Fraunhofer had designed an audio format better suited than any before to high-speed transmission and immediate access across widely distributed spatial expanses. Like the audio equivalent of a shipping container, the mp3 was created with one particular purpose in mind: to easily and conveniently transport anonymous packages of acoustic information from one place to another. No prior format was so perfectly amenable to being copied and shared.

In 1999, a student at Boston's Northeastern University released onto the internet a program called Napster which allowed the rapid distribution of mp3 files, to and from any node on a network, bypassing record shops, labels, and all the other standard trappings of distribution. In April of 2000, the Recording Industry Association of America sued to shut the service down. By that time, the company claimed to have some twenty-eight million users. Like the mythological hydra, as soon as this first peer-to-peer file-sharing head was cut off, dozens more sprung up to replace it: LimeWire, Kazaa, Gnutella, Scour, Grokster, Bearshare, eDonkey2000, and so on.

A year before Bowie's interview, Apple released its iTunes software, followed a few months later by the portable iPod player. The mp3 was embodied in a highly recognisable handheld device with unprecedented storage capacity. It was sleek and smooth and looked vaguely futuristic. Compared to a record, a tape, or a CD which might hold, at best, a few dozen different tracks, the iPod could carry over a thousand songs. This was a whole world of music, in your pocket.

Reading the *New York Times* piece, it's not entirely clear how Bowie felt about these developments. "The absolute transformation of everything that we ever thought about music will take place within ten years, and nothing is going to be able to stop it," he says. "You'd better be prepared for doing a lot of touring because that's really the only unique situation that's going to be left."

And then he says, "It's terribly exciting." But I'm not totally convinced he really felt so excited by the prospect of spending the rest of his life touring relentlessly. He was, then, a fifty-five year-old man with a one year-old child. In fact, two years later, he would cease touring altogether, for good. "But on the other hand," he says in the *Times* interview, "it doesn't matter if you think it's exciting or not; it's what's going to happen."

Bowie's rhetoric reminds me of a scene from a little later in *Impostor*. Gary Sinise's character, Spencer Olham, is on the run, suspected of being an alien spy. As he hurries through the dystopian future city, we glimpse huge propaganda posters hanging in the streets, bearing the slogans of the totalitarian government of 2079. "Unity Through Victory," says one. Another, draped ominously at the end of a long dark alley, says, "There Is No Alternative."

3.2 Taste-Mate

In the early 2000s we were always being told that there was no alternative. That this was it. Music was free now and we had better get used to it. Adapt or die. And this, we were told, was a good thing. Musicians had apparently been liberated from the monopolistic control of the major record labels. But for those of us who grew up in England during the government of Margaret Thatcher, the phrase "there is no alternative" has a different ring to it.

"There really is no alternative," Thatcher said to a press conference in June of 1980, defending the economic policies she took over from Friedrich Hayek's friends at the Mont Pelerin Society, which saw the gap between rich and poor in Britain widen into a yawning chasm during her reign. "We now have no alternative," she said again, at the Lord Mayor's Banquet in November of the same year, to hobbling the unions and crippling the welfare state. And again, she affirmed in January 1981, there was "no alternative" to closing Britain's coal mines, leading to the redundancy of some 173,000 workers, leaving whole communities decimated, never to recover.

By the end of her term in office, the phrase had become

indelibly associated with Margaret Thatcher. People called her Tina, after the phrase's acronym. And by the turn of the millennium, protestors against neo-liberal globalisation policies had taken to holding placards insisting pointedly that, on the contrary, "there is an alternative" and "another world is possible." But even as the thousands taking to the streets in Madrid, Seattle, London, Washington, and Genoa affirmed its negation, the notion that no other choice was possible was being promoted from a very different corner.

Typical in this sense was a 2005 book by Gerd Leonhard and David Kusek called *The Future of Music*. Attempts to limit the tide of unfettered online distribution were doomed to fail, the authors claimed; "the genie is already out of the bottle. There is no turning back to a time when the music could have been 'mechanically' protected."

The recalcitrant genie was a favoured image at the time. Already, in April of 2001, *Billboard* magazine had used the same metaphor when they assessed the latest file-sharing statistics, a year after the RIAA took Napster to court. "It looks like mp3 file-sharing is still quite active," they quoted industry analyst Phil Leigh. "The genie is out of the bottle and growing bigger everyday." But while *Billboard*'s interviewee was bemoaning the persistence of mp3 piracy, Kusek and Leonhard's *The Future of Music* is actually proposing something subtly different. Not quite free, but "what feels like free."

What they were arguing for, effectively, is something that, after Spotify, Deezer, and Tidal, is increasingly familiar today. None of those companies existed in 2005 when Leonhard and Kusek were writing. But the basic idea had been around at least since 1994, when the Stanford law professor Paul Goldstein wrote an influential study called *Copyright's Highway*. Goldstein pictured the music of the future beaming down from a "technology-packed satellite orbiting thousands of miles above the earth." With just a touch of 1950s nostalgia, he called it the "celestial jukebox," promising it would give "tens of millions of people access to a vast range of films, sound recordings, and printed material, awaiting only a subscriber's electronic command."

The idea was already gaining in popularity even as *Billboard* wrung its hands over the pirates. An article in *Salon* from November 2000 pictured the same "celestial jukebox" as a device you could hold in your hand or keep in your pocket. "Let's say you paid $150 for this device, and maybe $10–$20 a month as a flat subscription fee for access to the music – cheap at the price, considering that the average consumer now spends somewhere around $70 a year on music." There's something wrong with the maths there. Even putting aside the likelihood that your "$150 device" would probably have to be repurchased every few years, ten to twenty dollars times twelve months still works out as significantly more than seventy per year.

This should hardly be surprising. For all the divine associations of a phrase like "celestial jukebox," it's really just a form of rentier capitalism. As Patrick Burkart and Tom McCourt note in their book *Digital Music Wars*, "The record oligopoly's shift from goods to services via online delivery ... creates a new dependency between consumers (as renters) and corporations (as landlords)." The freedom promised by the disruptive force of the mp3 and Napster has quickly turned into a new form of exploitation under which consumers no longer pay once to enjoy as many times as they like, but must instead pay again and again, on a monthly basis, producing more and more profit for the new digital landlords. The authors of *The Future of Music* were well aware of this, and they predicted their "service" model would double or even triple the size of the music industry. So far, however, it's mostly just been profiting the technology conglomerates and telecommunication companies.

Kusek and Leonhard's book opens with a scene much like the one in *Impostor*. "It's 2015 and you wake to a familiar tune playing softly," they write. "You step into the shower and your personalized music program is ready for you, cued up with a new live version of a track you downloaded the other day. It is even better than the original recording, so while you dress, you tell your 'Taste-Mate' program to include the new track in your playlist rotation."

The fantasy continues with "Taste-Mates" and "Media Minders" seamlessly allocating appropriate aural stimulus from dawn till dusk, until finally, as the day draws to a close, Leonhard and Kusek picture their user winding down "with some New-Age derivatives of some of Mozart's original compositions, which you discovered late one night while cruising through the music sharing channels..."

"Music," they conclude, "will be like water: ubiquitous and free flowing." It's an image the authors attribute to that David Bowie interview in the *New York Times* from 2002. But the idea is actually much older, almost as old as running water itself. And it was imbued, from the very beginning, with all sorts of utopian expectations.

3.3 Golden Age

In 1832 there was an outbreak of cholera in Paris. Twenty thousand people died out of a population of sixty-five hundred thousand. It would be another two decades before a doctor in London realised the culprit was the city's unsanitary water supply. But the members of the Saint-Simonian "family," from their commune in the working-class suburb of Ménilmontant, were quick to propose a more radical solution to what they diagnosed as a year of "colère et de cholera." Charles Duveyrier, one of the youngest and most radical of the group, suggested nothing short of the destruction and rebuilding of the whole town centre.

In a prophetic fantasy penned that October, he pictured a future Paris reconstructed in the form of a human body. At the heart of the city was to stand a great temple in the shape of a woman. This was to be no ordinary church. Duveyrier imagined a temple of sound, dominated by a vast organ with pipes built of precious metals. From this instrument, he would send "a sweet and resounding music" through the man-city's "limbs of brass and stone" to every home, even to the very edge of the metropolis. At a time when even the water supply was not so well managed (hence all the cholera), Duveyrier was already proposing to pass sound through the same conduits. Here was piped music, nineteenth-century style.

Claude Henri de Rouvroy, the comte de Saint-Simon, was not quite thirty when the Bastille was stormed. By the time of Napoleon's coup, he was as though reborn, having dropped all his aristocratic titles, now styling himself as a valiant defender of what he referred to as "the most numerous and poorest class." He advocated the wholesale reorganisation of society from the top down according to scientific principles, believing the progress of society was a factor of its increasing organisation and specialisation. Like many nineteenth-century theorists, Saint-Simon regarded history according to a series of successive stages – in this case, twelve, of which, he believed, we had already reached the eleventh. The true "golden age," as he put it, lay just "ahead of us."

But before he died, Saint-Simon's last book, the *Nouveau Christianisme*, seemed to contain an abrupt volte-face. From arguing for the disinvestment of religious authority, he now spoke of "regenerating Christianity." For the sake of such a cause he hoped "to persuade artists, learned men, and chiefs of industry, that their interests were essentially the same as those of the mass of the people; that they belonged to the class of labourers, at the same time that they were natural chiefs."

In the very last months of his life, Saint-Simon and his increasingly devoted disciples collectively authored the *Opinions littéraires, philosophiques et industrielles*. A lengthy section attributed to Léon Halévy, younger brother to the composer Jacques Fromenthal Halévy, gives an even greater role to artists in the new society – they were to be its *"avant-garde"*. With this first known instance of this particular metaphor being applied to the arts, it retained much of the meaning it had in its military usage. As Halévy intended it, the avant-garde was less about being a superior elite than a kind of scouting party, forging ahead, clearing the path, and heralding the battalions that were to follow.

In 1832, the increasingly cult-like *"famille saint-simonien"* was in the midst of a recruitment drive – and, following the lead of Saint-Simon himself, artists, musicians in particular, were their prime targets. "Artists and poets," they pleaded. "Come to us without mistrust!" Among those they briefly drew towards the movement were such notable composers as Felicien David, Ferdinand Hiller, Franz Liszt, and Hector Berlioz. Berlioz had written to Duveyrier the previous year, pledging his full support for the "Saint-Simonian's plan" to reorganise society, and promising to "let you know my ideas about the ways in which you can use me musically."

Musical life in the Ménilmontant house where the Saint-Simonian inner circle lived together was clearly pretty active at this time. There were soirées and choral meetings, attempts to glorify the "Great Work" in song or rewrite the *Marseillaise*. There seems even to have been an idea to compose some sort of opera on a Saint-Simonian theme, most likely with a libretto by Duveyrier, who had been appointed in-house *chef de musique* (despite little apparent instrumental ability). But despite Berlioz's plans at this time for an oratorio under the apocalyptic title of *Le Dernier Jour du monde* about a "few worthies" and their prophet struggling against a corrupt state in the last days of the earth – chiming almost perfectly with the somewhat paranoid self-mythology of the Saint-Simonians at this time – nothing appears to have come of it.

Nonetheless Saint-Simon and his followers exerted a considerable influence on both the musical and utopian currents of the later nineteenth century, even as they hemmed so close to Charles Fourier's ideas that he threatened to sue. In England, the *Nouveau Christianisme* was translated by James Smith, who acted as editor to the industrial reformer Robert Owen, and contemporary observers would see in Owen's cooperative and socialist experiments an "Englishification" of Saint-Simonism. Liszt's position (and subsequent *Zukunftsmusik*-ing) at Weimar are practically unthinkable without his brief flush of enthusiasm for the Saint-Simonian doctrine in the 1830s. What is less often remarked upon is the persistence of Duveyrier's fantasy of sound-bearing tubes, carrying symphonic strains from a central distribution point to every home, as an image of networked dissemination in a technologically-advanced utopia of music.

When the French poet Théophile Gautier returned from the Great Exhibition in London in 1851, he was clearly inspired by the cult of industrial progress he had encountered there. Come December he would publish an article in the newspaper *Le Pays* entitled 'Paris Futur'. It bore distinct resemblances to Duveyrier's 'Ville Nouvelle' – not least in its opening pledge to "steam-roller over present day Paris." In a passage recalling at once the London Exhibition's congress of the works of all nations and the Saint-Simonian *temple universel*, the author proposes for his reconstructed capital, one great "hybrid temple" to include "all the architectures of the past, present, and future." The organ of this vast church would pump specially-composed music throughout the city through "pipes as long as the column in the Place Vendôme."

Albert Robida's *Le Vingtième Siècle*, from 1883, then comes along as something of a transitional work. Its hero, M. Ponto, receives his opera direct to his domestic telephonoscope, by "wire." But, the author notes, those theatres too small to maintain their own orchestra are able to store music transmitted from the larger houses "in tubes until the stage prompter turns on the valve in his box." In fact, the apparent distinction between aqueous pipes and electrical wires is probably more illusory than real. The family, after all, has its instrumental music "delivered electrically through pipes" – a salutary reminder that electricity, in the late nineteenth century, was itself conceived of as a sort of liquid that might flow down a tube as gravity dictates.

Robida's piped music no longer issues from a central church, as in the Saint-Simonian dream, but a centralised corporation. "The Great Music Company factory now stands as a music monopoly in Paris," Robida tells us. "The musician, this plague of last century, this omnipresent and neurotic species rightly nicknamed 'the cholera of salons,' fortunately has become extinct. The last survivors, a dozen in number, practice their art at the factory." The reference was pointed. By 1883, everyone knew what caused cholera, and Paris had spent the previous few decades undertaking a major overhaul of its public sanitation and water supply. Just as the new water pipes would eradicate the cholera of the Parisian bowel, so Robida's musical pipes would clear up the cholera infecting French salons.

Still, some trace of the Saint-Simonian art-religion would persist in Edward Bellamy's popular utopian novel of 1888, *Looking Backward*, in which a young American named Julian West falls asleep in the nineteenth century and wakes up in the year 2000 to find a world of nationalised industry and radically redistributed wealth. Co-operation has replaced competition and everyone is the better for it. In the future Boston foreseen by Bellamy, the people receive their music and religious sermons alike via the same telephonic wires. Every home has its dedicated "music room" in which to enjoy both their favourite songs and their Sunday mass. Either way, people listen just as raptly. Symphony and sanctity pass through the same media and each commands the same devoted reception. No-one need want for sonic succour. The pipes, now, were calling for a new democracy of music.

3.4 Telharmonium

"Come, then, into the music room," ushers the demure Edith Leete to an increasingly befuddled Julian West in a scene roughly midway through Edward Bellamy's *Looking Backward*. Upon entering this room of polished wood, West, having only recently awakened from a hundred years' sleep and still a little groggy, is surprised to find no new musical instruments or anything that "by any stretch of the imagination could be conceived as such." Instead, Edith, his guide to the new world of the future, offers him a sort of menu card. At the mere touch of "one or two screws," he finds the room at once "filled with music," from no apparent source.

"There is nothing in the least mysterious about the music," Edith reassures him. "We have simply carried the idea of labor saving by cooperation into our musical service as into everything else. There are a number of music rooms in the city, perfectly adapted acoustically to the different sorts of music. These halls are connected by telephone with all the houses of the city whose people care to pay the small fee, and there are none, you may be sure, who do not."

This very "music room" passage from *Looking Backward* was quoted in full in a brochure produced some twenty years later. The pamphlet's purpose was to advertise a new invention regarded as the fulfilment of Bellamy's vision. It was called the telharmonium, and it was the twentieth century's first machine for the drawing of music directly from electricity. It used an alternating current to produce sine tones which could be controlled and combined by a keyboard and a number of tone wheels. At a time when the phonograph, like the recently invented pianola, was still seen to offer nothing but "canned" mechanical music; the telharmonium promised a live experience, supremely sensitive to the expressive tendencies of its performer.

The inventor, a former Iowa court stenographer named Thaddeus Cahill, regarded his machine as an attempt to rectify what he saw as the "defects" of the piano, violin, and organ: the three hitherto most common tools of domestic music-making. One lacked sustain, the other lacked the ability to produce chords, the third was insufficiently expressive. The telharmonium would master all three. In the press, it was championed as a kind of super-instrument, capable of imitating the sounds of *all* other instruments at once, along with many entirely novel sounds of its own. But for Ray Stannard Baker, writing in *McClure's Magazine* in July 1906 (an article quoted extensively in the same promotional brochure that excerpted *Looking Backward*), the telharmonium promised nothing less than "a new era of music, what may be called, indeed, the democracy of music."

Cahill's invention offered a novel means not just of producing musical tones, but also of distributing them. After all, the signal already had to pass by wire from the keyboard to the dynamo to the speaker cone – why stop there? "Buy music by meter like gas or water" promised the headline of the *Chicago Examiner*. For just a few cents a day, subscribers could receive music in their homes direct by wire, just like Bellamy's telephonic service. The difference was that in *Looking Backward*, much like Robida's *Vingtième Siècle*, there remained the presumption of some live concert actually taking place somewhere that was then broadcast to people's homes. With the telharmonium, no such original live event existed. At the moment of music's electrification, it became pure transmission, a copy without an original, existing only for the moment of its dissemination.

For journalists like Baker there was a kind of metonymic substitution at work: in the actual provision of just one detail from Bellamy's utopia, the whole system is implied by synecdoche. "Dr. Cahill's new invention suggests, if it does not promise," goes the *McClure's Magazine* piece, "a complete change in the system by which a comparatively few rich people enjoy the best music to the exclusion of all the others."

But the telharmonium was also a vast industrial enterprise. The instrument itself weighed two hundred tons and consisted of a sixty-foot mainframe built of eighteen-inch steel girders. In its presence, Baker felt "the impression of nothing so much as a busy machine-shop, or the centre of a considerable manufacturing industry." The enterprise was patronised by wealthy industrialists and philanthropists like Westinghouse and Peabody. Its business was promoted in New York by a railway magnate. If this was sonic socialism, it was socialism of a very peculiar kind.

The ambition, ultimately, was to become a media conglomerate – perhaps the first media conglomerate dedicated to music – offering electrical symphonies via telephone wires to subscribers throughout the country. But with the Panic of 1907, as the New York Stock Exchange saw fifty percent fall off its share values, the telharmonium fell too. Its business never recovered and its promised "democracy of music" never arrived.

Cahill had clearly borne high hopes for his device though. Speaking at a lecture to the Music Teachers' National Association at Columbia University in November 1907, even as his company was on the verge of bankruptcy, Cahill made bold claims for the musical possibilities materialised by the telharmonium. "The composer of the past," he began, "has been like the chemist or alchemist of ancient time, who could use in his combinations some few compound bodies only. The composer of the future will have in the sinusoidal vibrations of electrical music those pure elements out of which all tone-compounds can be built; not merely the known and approved tones of the orchestra, but many shades and nuances heretofore unattainable."

But despite the enthusiastic approval from across the Atlantic of Ferruccio Busoni, who deemed it "an extraordinary electrical invention for producing scientifically perfect music," the telharmonium was never employed in the production of new sounds, or new music of any sort. Demonstration concerts at the company's "Telharmonium Hall" and elsewhere were invariably programmed to suit the tastes of potential investors. Rossini's *William Tell* overture was a perennial favourite, as were selections from Mendelssohn, Brahms, and extracts from Italian operas. The machine was finally dismantled and sold for scrap before any serious composer could get their hands on it.

What Cahill's machine did herald, however, was the return of a kind of music that the nineteenth century had sought strenuously to eradicate. Wagner is said to have witheringly dismissed Mozart's instrumental works with the remark that he sometimes fancied he could hear the clatter of the Emperor's dinnerware interfering with the music. In his time, the major reforms of the Opéra de Paris were largely directed towards turning the theatre into a place where the bourgeois might listen to music in silent concentration, as opposed to a place for upper-class socialising which also happened to play music. But Cahill and his business associates saw the unprecedented numbers of people then gathering socially in urban public spaces and recognised a potential audience for background music.

In 1907, an article in *Gunter's Magazine* featured an artist's impression of the "dinner of the future," at which telharmonic music would be broadcast from an overhead lamp throughout the meal. In the same year, the new Plaza Hotel had every room wired to receive telharmonium broadcasts that would never arrive. Further plans were made to broadcast music in factories, dentists' waiting rooms, and barber shops. All of these plans indicate a particular listening situation, one in which listening is no longer centre-stage but more like an ambient adjunct to some other more pressing activity, whether eating, working, or getting a haircut. The solemn attention of Edward Bellamy's "music room" was now out the window. The peculiar modern phenomenon of people playing music but not really listening to it starts here.

Few of these schemes came to fruition. Those that did were not very successful. As the French composer Erik Satie discovered – when, around the same time, he attempted to present his "furniture music" to the public – people were too entrained. Satie wanted to write melodies that would slink back and form "part of the noises of the environment." But music was still sufficiently rare a thing. The urban bourgeoisie who were the target audience for both Satie and Cahill were not yet the jaded aristocrats of the *ancien régime* when it came to music. People still tended to shut up and listen to it (much to Satie's frustration).

But an officer of the U.S. Signal Corps called George Owen Squier was clearly paying attention. In 1922, he created a company called Wired Radio, which offered a music subscription service, by telephone wire, direct to people's homes. It was not, at first, terribly successful. But in 1934, inspired by George Eastman's Kodak Company, Squier changed the company name to Muzak. The core of the business was restructured towards serving workplaces, rather than homes. By the 1950s it was the biggest consumer of phone lines in the whole world.

3.5 Stimulus Progression

Muzak's path to domination of the telephone network was never a smooth one. For a long time they believed that what they were offering was simply a different medium, that the same music could be presented by different means. After all, using the new "multiplexing" technique developed by George Squier, sounds could be transmitted down the telephone wire at much higher quality than was then offered by the radio – and radio was seen as the main competitor. The company spent loads of money recording the popular artists of the day, which at that time was mostly swing orchestras. Muzak's archives held some of the few original recordings of jazz harpist Casper Reardon. They held very little that sounded specifically Muzak-y. All that changed with the arrival of Harold Burris-Meyer.

Burris-Meyer began as a consultant, on loan from the Stevens Institute of Technology. Before long he would rise to become vice-president of the company. His wartime research with Richard Cardinell into music in the workplace laid the foundations for what would become Muzak's own distinctive sound. Afterwards, they would no longer see their biggest competitor as the radio, but silence itself.

Based on experiments in armaments factories, Cardinell and Burris-Meyer came up with a series of best practices for the supply of music to work by: "Avoid identifiable vocalists or tricky instrumental music … Provide bright, snappy music at start of work and just before daily fatigue points … Don't play music louder than is necessary for good definition … Select music so as to create a progressive mood, building up intensity and tempo from operetta to waltz to foxtrot." These recommendations, outlined in a 1944 article for *Popular Science* magazine, became the basis of Muzak's "stimulus progression" programme, rolled out by Burris-Meyer during his vice-presidency in the mid to late Forties.

"Stimulus progression" was a subtle means of manipulating a worker's sense of time. Alternating every fifteen minutes with blocks of silence, the music was programmed according to an "ascending curve" of intensity, developing from more subdued to more stimulating sounds. The idea was that it would countermand the average employee's "fatigue curve." Tracks were meticulously categorised according to a scale ranging from "Gloomy – minus three" to "Ecstatic – plus eight." Within each half-hour rotation of sound and silence, three-minute-long tracks would vary in mood, building up energy and gently guiding the rhythms of work. The passage of the music sought to replace the natural temporal cues of the passing day. In this way, what might otherwise seem like a long expanse of time, occupied by an endless repetition of the same mindless task, could be broken up into manageable chunks. Time became cyclical, instead of progressive.

Muzak had found its groove, its unique identifying mark. If you imagine the sound of Muzak, the sounds that spring to mind will most likely recall the stimulus progression recordings of the mid-twentieth century: angelic choirs in major keys, silken strings and muted brass, all in a gurgling mid-tempo. But being so recognisable, it was wide open to attack. In 1948, the local transport company in Washington D.C. began broadcasting "music as you ride" supplied by Muzak on its buses and trams. Despite its popularity with some ninety percent of those polled, however, a campaign was staged to get rid of it – eventually going all the way to the Supreme Court.

The case was lost and Muzak stayed on the buses, but hackles had clearly been raised. Over the course of the campaign, *The Washington Post* printed hundreds of letters complaining about this piped music. Still, Harold Burris-Meyer simply smiled and shook his head. "If people who claim they require absolute silence were placed in a near vacuum," he said in a *Reader's Digest* interview at the time, "they would probably go nuts." (As an occasional naval advisor on psychoacoustic matters, it's possible that he was speaking here from first-hand knowledge).

It didn't end there. By the 1970s, films like *Dawn of the Dead* and *The Stepford Wives* would present Muzak as the ultimate expression of mindless consumerism. The scene in George Romero's 1978 zombie masterpiece where its undead suburbanites shuffle through an abandoned shopping mall, staggering through the concourse and collapsing into water fountains to the sound of massed strings and plinky-plonk percussion, was a perfect pastiche of late-capitalist ennui. In 1986, rock dinosaur Ted Nugent made a very public offer to buy the whole company for ten million dollars – just so he could "destroy it."

Muzak turned him down. But they were beginning to recognise they might just have a bit of an image problem. More concerted campaign groups were forming with names like Mu-Sick and Pipedown. The latter, which boasts of successfully petitioning Gatwick Airport and Waterstones bookshop to remove their background music, has a quote from the actor Stephen Fry on their website: "Piped water, piped electricity, piped gas," he says,

"– but never piped music!"

By 1997 Muzak had ditched stimulus progression entirely in favour of a new programme consisting entirely of original artists playing their own songs. Over the following decade they licensed a phenomenal catalogue of familiar tunes. Seven hundred and seventy-five Beatles recordings, one hundred and thirty by Kanye West, three hundred and twenty-four by Led Zeppelin, eighty-four by Gwen Stefani, a hundred and ninety-one by 50 Cent, and nine hundred and eighty-three by Miles Davis. Having shrugged off its signature style, it was no longer possible to tell by listening to a single piece of music whether it was Muzak or not. What made the company distinctive was not the sound of a specific track, but the sequencing of songs together; the way they conspired to contribute to a particular mood or delineate the features of a particular brand. As the McGill University professor Jonathan Sterne wrote in his study of the "aural architecture" of the Mall of America, "all recorded music is at least potentially Muzak."

And it worked – for a while. By 2004 they could boast that their piped selections were heard by a hundred million people every day, across dozens of major retail outlets, from the Gap to McDonalds to Barnes & Noble. "What does your business sound like?" asked the glossily rebranded company brochures. For a while the answer seemed inevitable: it sounds like Muzak (whatever it is).

Then in February 2009, less than six months after a little Swedish start-up called Spotify launched its platform onto the internet, Muzak filed for bankruptcy, citing one hundred and five million dollars of missed debt repayments. It seemed to be the end of the line for the company, just shy of its ninetieth birthday. But maybe the Ted Nugents of this world shouldn't be so quick to celebrate. The Muzak company may have died but its principles seem to have been generalised to society at large.

"Our days are filled with listening," notes Anahid Kassabian in her recent book *Ubiquitous Listening*, "ubiquitous musics come out of the wall, our televisions, our video games, our computers, and even out of our clothing (see, for examples, the range of clothing with pockets for mp3 players and sleeves for ear-phone cords, or Oakley-Thump, the world's first digital music eyewear, or temperature-regulating ski jackets). Workplaces, shops, homes, cars, buses, trains, phones, restaurants, clubs... music is everywhere, some through our own choices, some without our sanction or control."

Kassabian notes that we have developed a new kind of hearing in order to cope with music's now-inescapable omnipresence. Her concept of "ubiquitous listening" – a kind of "secondary" listening, a listening "alongside" – is quite independent of what style or genre of music is in question; it is a product rather of its sourcelessness. Ubiquitous listening is in the very nature of a sound coming "from everywhere and nowhere." It is a product of music's status as transmission. The mp3 is the perfect counterpart to this new mode of listening. They are "symbiotic," as Jonathan Sterne argues; "the so-called mp3 revolution had made more music more ready-to-hand for more people than at any other time in human history." It is a format, he claims, tailor-made for listening alongside other activities. It "is designed for casual users," he writes. The way it compresses sound is predicated on the gaps in our hearing in a "normal" listening environment – that is, one in which there is a bunch of other stuff going on: traffic, air conditioning, the washing up, the general hubbub of other people talking.

At the same time that Muzak was amassing its vast catalogue of original artist records, students and DJs and music fans of all stripes were doing exactly the same thing – only they weren't paying for it. The mp3 had found its characteristic expression, its raison d'être. Taking up such a minuscule amount of actual physical room, it could be sent around the world in seconds and stored for ages without regard for the space it took up. "It's difficult to describe to people ... how much material was suddenly available," digital rights activist John Perry Barlow recalls in a 2013 documentary about the history of Napster.

I remember the days well. Friends stuffing their hard drives with as many songs as they could, endlessly trawling through Kazaa or Limewire for every last b-side by obscure post-rock groups, bootlegged live recordings of quasi-mythical audio saints. Legendary lost recordings were lost no more, and being found, ceased also to be legendary. Every scrap of acoustic evidence was amassed and made available. Welcome to the panaudicon.

"I'm closing in on ninety-five gigabytes of music," admitted American critic Karla Starr in a blog for the *Phoenix New Times*, "much of it never listened to." Like the Muzak catalogue, these songs were no longer really there to be listened to, more to define sets of boundaries and articulate an identity. The finer distinctions of taste were defined by mass measured in bits, by completeness as a mark of dedicated excavation work.

The science-fiction author Cory Doctorow, in a foreword to the book *Sound Unbound*, described the careful management of the musical files on his own personal music player. "I've rated every track from one to five," he said. "I start every day with my playlist of four- to five-star music that I haven't heard in thirty days, like making sure that I visit all my friends at least once a month... After that, I listen to songs I haven't rated, and rate them. Then it's on to four- to five-star songs I've heard fewer than five times, total. I don't want random shuffle: I want directed, optimised shuffle."

Doctorow's optimised shuffle sounds like the point where stimulus progression meets the operationalised algorithms of artificial intelligence, where all pleasure, all caprice has been subordinated to a bureaucratic work ethic. I don't know if Doctorow actually programmed some sort of automated bot to do that sorting for him and pick out his daily listening like a doting parent choosing clothes for their child, but he surely could have done. It couldn't be that hard. What, then, does that imply about the degrees of meaningfulness different music holds for him on a daily basis?

To Erik Davis, techgnostic theorist of the digital counterculture, Doctorow's careful parsing sounds more like "data-processing" than music-listening. "The more we deal with recorded music in the form of digital files," Davis writes in a column for *Arthur* magazine, "the more that music takes on the characteristics of data, and the more its specific qualities as music melt into that multimedia torrent of bits that keep us chained to our screens. From a new media perspective, this breakdown sounds kind of cool and futuristic, and it certainly opens up new possibilities of expression and intervention. But I'm not sure these transformations really support deep and engaged listening."

When Lejaren Hiller and Leonard Isaacson treated musical notes as informational bits to be processed, randomised, and reconfigured in their *Illiac Suite* of 1956, it was greeted by the press as a sci-fi curiosity – music composed by a "mechanical brain." Few people today would listen to a random stream of notes, tweaked here and there to produce the "right" kind of data (yes, some people do, but not so many). There is a feeling that something is lost when composition is reduced to the mechanical process of shuffling a deck of cards. We have a kind of psychological resistance – especially when we know that's how it was made. But when it comes to choosing between different pieces of music, picking which song to listen to and when, we seem to be much more comfortable. The random processing of one's music collection, the arbitrary assignment of a given soundtrack to a given experience, is built into one of the most popular devices for storing, transporting, and listening to music in the world: the iPod.

Sociologist Michael Bull has written extensively about what he calls "iPod culture." In his 2007 book *Sound Moves*, Bull compares the rapturous "polyrhythmic" descriptions of early twentieth-century urban life by the likes of Robert Musil, Joseph Roth, and Henri Lefebvre, with the responses of his own interviewees. Take "Tracy," an enthusiastic iPod user who describes using music to filter out the intruding voices of Mexican immigrants as she does her shopping. Or "Ivan," who says his iPod makes it "easier to avoid guilt-inducing encounters with the homeless." This kind of "auditory filtering," Bull claims, is "a central strategy of iPod users" who use the device to create what one interviewee calls his very own "privacy bubble."

Within each sonic bubble, the iPod becomes not just a music player but a kind of therapeutic tool. "I keep some slow music that gives me a calm, peaceful feeling when I'm in busy or chaotic settings, like on the subway," says one of Bull's interviewees. Another speaks of a specific mix of Eighties pop "that wakes me up and gets me motivated for my day." The spontaneous practice of iPod users comes to very closely resemble the model developed by Richard Cardinell and Harold Burris-Meyer back in the Forties. "Bright, snappy music at start of work and just before daily fatigue points." Like Muzak, iPod culture instrumentalises music in the service of capitalist rationality. It becomes less a source of pleasure and aesthetic contemplation, more a kind of mood regulator to turn listeners into fit and productive workers.

We dose ourselves with sound, self-medicating with music. Every playlist becomes the perfect stimulus progression programme, expertly tailored to suit brand you. Work time is no longer measured by the supervisor's stopwatch. It is deftly controlled and micro-managed by workers themselves, each inhabiting a privatised temporal bubble both empowering and isolating.

3.6 Blip Included

There's a funny story in a 2012 piece by Tom Lamont for *The Guardian*, about the legacy of Napster. It takes place a few years after the service fell silent, while its spoils still lingered on in many an iTunes library. "On a long drive through California, I put on a homemade CD of mostly legitimately bought mp3s plus a few old Napster downloads," Lamont begins. "There were three Americans in the car, and when Steppenwolf's grand road-trip anthem, 'Magic Carpet Ride', came on we all sang along–sang along, too, when a mechanical blip interrupted the chorus. Nobody could believe it. Years before, on computers thousands of miles apart, we'd all downloaded the same corrupted mp3 and got to know Steppenwolf with blip included."

I like this story because it speaks about the way the specific artefacts of a particular medium can contribute to the emotional resonances we maintain about a piece of music. Record collectors may grow misty-eyed over the crackle of a vinyl run-out groove, but it's unusual to hear such an evocation of nostalgia relating to a technology that is still as young and widely-used as the mp3.

I also like it because it reminds me of another story John Cage used to tell. "I was present at a concert conducted by Stravinsky, of one of his own works," the composer recalls in a segment from Peter Greenaway's film *Four American Composers*. "And I was sitting behind a ten year-old child and his father. Then after the performance was finished, the child turned to his father and said, 'That isn't the way it goes!'"

For Cage, the anecdote proves that records give people a distorted idea of music, a false impression of fixity. The boy heard Stravinsky's interpretation of his own piece as wrong because he'd heard it differently on a record. By objectifying the piece in a particular way, that record, the boy presumably reasoned, had set down for good how it was *supposed* to go. What he knew was not the piece itself, but its instantiation on a particular recording. But for Cage, a piece of music is a living thing and the authority over "the way it goes" remains invested in the composer.

Cage's attitude towards records seems sort of quaint now—even paradoxical, since he used records and record players in several of his performances and, by some estimates, he was one of the twentieth century's most recorded composers. But, though he often said similar sorts of things, they weren't always one hundred percent consistent. At its most nuanced, Cage's position comes close to what critics of fine art would call "medium specificity." Clement Greenberg, in an oft-cited essay from 1960 called 'Modernist Painting' had argued that the "unique and proper area of competence of each art coincided with all that was unique in the nature of its medium." Just a few years earlier, in 1957, Cage had spoken of using tape "not simply to record performances of music but to make a new music that was possible only because of it."

One needn't necessarily read Greenberg's and Cage's statements as normative, as injunctions to operate in a particular way. For a long time, artists—sculptors, perhaps, in particular—have been conscious of a need to be sensitive to their materials. In his book *Music and the Myth of Wholeness*, the composer and improviser Tim Hodgkinson even suggests that "what distinguishes artistic making as such from, say, making a useful tool is that artistic work doesn't treat materials as inert and simply to be knocked into shape, or as icons of economic value or usefulness, but rather as stuff whose given texture and structure has to be perceptually engaged with – stuff that, if you look at it the right way, has a magnetism of its own, irrespective of any other kind of value."

When it comes to wood or stone, I suspect few people would take issue with this statement. But for most of the twentieth century, the material stuff of music, as far as most listeners were concerned, was not abstract tones dancing in space or dots and lines on a page. It was magnetic tape or the grooves on a vinyl disc or radio waves passing through the air. Composers could choose to ignore that or engage with it. But if they chose the former, they probably shouldn't be too surprised if most listeners failed to understand them.

The Muzak Corporation took more than twenty years to find its unique and proper area of competence. It had never made much sense for them to present music in the same manner as the radio since their means of dissemination were so different. Radio, as a one-to-many broadcast system, always presents itself as another space intruding into the domestic environment—or rather, as a profusion of different spaces. Perhaps the quintessential radio experience, the source of its most unique thrills, is of turning the dial from one station to the next, switching from the local station down the road, to the national station a hundred miles away, and perhaps a foreign station broadcasting from across the sea, or a "pirate" channel somewhere in the middle of that sea. Successful radio music tends to make an immediate play for the listener's attention in order to arrest the impulse to keep turning the dial. Silence is anathema.

The most effective works for radio—whether that's Elvis Presley singing 'Mystery Train', Orson Welles's notorious adaptation of *The War of the Worlds*, or Stockhausen's *Gesang der Jünglinge* (composed in the studios of the Westdeutcher Rundfunk and able to captivate the attention of a young György Ligeti even in the midst of armed bombardment)—fabricate the experience of multiple different spaces, all competing for attention at once, cramming the peculiar thrill of twitching the dial into the space of a single work.

But Muzak sent its music by wire, like the telephone, the telephonoscope, and the telharmonium. Since telephone wires invariably led to a central exchange, the power to switch from one point on the network to another was never wholly in the hands of the consumer at home. This situation favoured a subscription model (which would have been very difficult to enforce over the radio waves), and therefore obviated the need for advertising or the kind of attention-grabbing tactics associated with radio. Muzak wasn't competing directly with any other alternative provider of wired music. As they realised themselves, their biggest competition was the absence of music altogether. So Muzak could integrate silence into its own programmes and in some respects even mimic the way "silence" operates (at least in the Cagean sense of sound you don't pay attention to).

Wired music, in fact, always worked best when it was treated like any other piped-in service, whether water, gas, or electricity. It was a tap that could be turned off or on at will to perform a specific function at a specific time, but was otherwise pretty much just part of the architecture of the building. Hence the term "aural architecture" that Muzak adopted in later years. It has never been a situation conducive to engaged listening.

Despite the attempts of early radio manufacturers to fashion their products after items of furniture, building them out of heavy, dark woods or fitting them into cabinets and chests and so forth, this was never really the way radio functioned in the home. It was always too captivating to be simply *there* in the way that a sofa or a fridge is just there. The kind of direct, almost intimate address that radio broadcasters use with their audiences would never have worked on a Muzak programme. Furniture doesn't command that kind of attention unless it's new, unfamiliar – or broken. Muzak, likewise (and it tried very hard never to sound new or unfamiliar).

In later years, as the sets got smaller and more portable, the radio was as likely to divide the home or work environment into distinct, semi-autonomous bubbles as to unify it. Everyone could choose their own station and listen independently, utterly absorbed in signals from a distinct, far-off space – even while sitting a few feet from someone captivated by a different space altogether. But Muzak imposed its rhythms on the whole workforce as one, simultaneously and indiscriminately.

Wired and wireless media both work to break up and fragment time, but in very different ways. The radio, with its bulletins, weather reports, and published schedules, worked according to an urgent real-time that was also a kind of national or universal time. Time, in fact, became standardised around the world with a series of pips broadcast wirelessly from the Eiffel Tower on the first of July 1913. But Muzak sought to eradicate external time altogether and impose its own structures in its place. Muzak's time was work time and that stopped having anything to do with real time with the industrial revolution.

Records were something different again, though it took a long time for anybody to realise that. Thomas Edison had initially conceived of his phonograph simply as a means of storing telephone conversations for later reference. The very name "phonograph" suggests some manner of written speech and this evidential quality was reflected in Edison's hope that the device would "provide invaluable records, instead of being the recipient of momentary and fleeting communication." We still fall into Edison's trap whenever we think of records as being just that: a material *record* of a real event. The inclination to refer to an album as "overproduced" is a sure symptom of this, since it suggests that the studio apparatus is intervening too noticeably between the listener and the performance. What it neglects to realise is that the performance itself is already a product of that apparatus through and through.

The truth is records practically never really fulfilled the function of a neutral document. Whether employed commercially to set down the voice of Enrico Caruso, or by ethnographers in the field capturing the songs of isolated tribes, the nature of the device ensured that performances inevitably had to be set up and staged specifically for its recording. They only ever bore scant relation to the event supposedly being "recorded," which in the actual instance only existed for the sake of its recording. But it wasn't really until the 1960s that anyone cared to exploit the medium specificity of recorded music. Afterwards, music would never be the same again.

3.7 Music Easel

In the early Sixties, Morton Subotnick had a vision of the future. "I did a piece in '61," he told me via Skype from his apartment in New York, "which I thought of as what would happen on the stage one hundred years from now." He could see the world around him was changing. Since the Second World War, cheap electronics had become pervasive as war surplus. Subotnick could see that music – and not *just* music – would be affected by this "in the same way that written language had when the printing press had been created."

The piece he presented in San Francisco that year was meant as a vision of what would become normal "after generations of people growing up with this technology." It was written for two stereo tape machines, their four speakers surrounding the audience, along with four musicians and a series of theatrical lighting flats upon which different-coloured lights and images could be projected and controlled by hand. Towards the end, Subotnick's friend, the poet Michael McClure, read some verses from his book, *Flowers of Politics*.

"The review came out and said something like, a new art form has been born!" Subotnick recalled. "So I thought, oh well, maybe

I have an aptitude to do something – and I *hated* the piece. So I decided, I'm gonna work on it and perfect this thing. It may take me ten, fifteen years. I don't know. And then I'll stop and do something else. I stopped in 1993. I finished it."

Subotnick knew he was onto something. But he didn't know quite what. The "new art form" touted by the review for this 1961 piece would, in the composer's view, find its fulfilment in *Jacob's Room*, a chamber opera first performed in Philadelphia in April 1993, collaging texts by Virginia Woolf, Plato, Moshe Kohn, Nicholas Gage, Alicia Partnoy, and Alexander Donat, scored for four cellos, synthesizers, and electronics, with visuals by the legendary video artists Steina and Woody Vasulka.

Jacob's Room is an extraordinary piece of work. But it probably goes without saying that, from the perspective of 2016, an opera using electronic sounds and visuals – though very welcome – does not clearly represent a revolution on a par with the printing press. That does not mean that the intuition Subotnick had in 1961, of an impending seismic shift in the way we use and understand music, was wrong.

For much of the Fifties, like most of his peers on the West Coast at that time – La Monte Young, James Tenney, Terry Riley, and so on – Subotnick had been composing in a style influenced by the twelve-tone technique of Arnold Schoenberg and his students. "My own version of post-Webern," he calls it now.

He had been a clarinettist since childhood. A doctor had prescribed taking up a wind instrument as a cure for a persistent cough. As a young adult, he would play for symphony orchestras and compose music for TV, theatre, dance, or pretty well anyone that would ask him. "I just wanted to write music," he told me. "I loved blank pages and then putting lines on it and it would turn into sound. That was magic to me. And if I could make a living doing it, I would do it."

One day he got a call from Herbert Blau, director of the local Actor's Workshop. They were doing a new version of *King Lear* with a twenty-six year-old Michael O'Sullivan in the lead. The whole thing was going to be "apocalyptic," Subotnick recalls. "It was going to take place in a kind of primordial humanity," he said, "and the sets and the costumes were made from seashells." The company were looking for "a wild composer." Subotnick had been recommended as just such a man.

"I thought, I don't want to write *incidental* music for a production like this. So I recorded Michael – Herb directed him – the way he was going to do the storm scene, a year in advance. I recorded it and made all the music from his voice. I cut and pasted and upside-down and backwards, fast and slow. It took me almost a year."

"But that's how I got there," he continued, "It was working on this for a year – I realised something that I had not thought of before then, which is that I really didn't like being on the stage. And I thought, well, this technology could create a new paradigm, a new environment for composing. It would be like painting. You would be composing music as a studio art."

Over the course of the rest of the decade, Subotnick would set the template for this new kind of composer. He worked tirelessly towards the creation of new compositional situations, uniquely suited to the tools of his time. "I had made the decision at that point," he told me, "that this new technology was going to allow for everything to be different." After reading the review of his 1961 piece for four loudspeakers, four musicians, and a poet, Subotnick put an ad in the paper. He was looking for an engineer. Someone who could help him build something that would be a little more user-friendly than the endless tape splices then necessary to make electronic music. The man who replied was Don Buchla, and together they would put together one of the world's first analogue synthesizers.

"I used as a model for myself the metaphor of Chopin and the piano," Subotnick said in another interview, for the *We Create Music* blog. "He used the concert grand in a way that just wouldn't have made sense as anything but solo piano pieces...I was looking for something equivalent with a record. What would a record be if [the piece] never got performed on the stage, just for the record?"

The opportunity to realise this dream came along one night in 1966, when a guy in a business suit stepped into Subotnick's Bleecker Street studio in New York, at about three in the morning. That man was Jac Holzmann, the founder of Elektra and Nonesuch Records, and he wanted Subotnick to make an LP. Over the course of the next thirteen months, Subotnick gradually shaped and formed a piece called *Silver Apples of the Moon*. It consisted of two movements, each one the length of a single side of twelve-inch vinyl. "For the first time," the album sleeve proclaimed, "an original full-scale composition has been created expressly for the record medium."

He put it together in a way that would have been practically impossible for any composer up to that point. He would improvise with Buchla's synthesizer and then listen to what he had done, taking each gesture at a time, then working with it, editing it, adding to it, reshaping it. "I thought of it like a painter's easel," Subotnick told me. "I had originally called [the synthesizer] an electronic music easel." To work like that, to have the kind of control, ease of gesture, and immediate feedback that a painter has, to become effectively composer, performer, and listener all at the same time, is commonplace now. But at the time it was unprecedented. What really surprised Subotnick, though, was what happened when it was first presented to the public.

3.8 Love in a UFO

Around '66, '67, Morton Subotnick seems to have been in his studio pretty well all the time. "I worked twelve to fourteen hours a day," he's said. People would pop by while he was working. He was right in Greenwich Village. The Bitter End and Cafe au Go Go were a stone's throw away. "People would come to my studio at two o'clock in the morning and just be there. Nobody introduced themselves," he told me. Somehow word had got around that this guy was making some pretty far-out noises in a studio on Bleecker Street. "I never met anyone. People just came to the studio. I didn't go out. I was just working all the time."

Two guys he did meet were Stan Freeman and Jerry Brandt. "They came into my studio," Subotnick recalls, "and they said, we just bought a name, 'The Electric Circus'. We don't know what an electric circus actually is. Everyone says we should come here and that you would tell us." He did.

The Electric Circus opened in July 1967 at the Dom on St. Mark's Place, the same place where Andy Warhol had held his 'Exploding Plastic Inevitable'. At Subotnick's suggestion, they had Don Buchla design the sound system and he put the sub-woofers right on the floor so people would feel the vibrations of the bass through their bodies. "The whole floor really rocked,"

Subotnick told me. "It literally did. You were, like, *inside* the speaker." Tony Martin, another old friend from San Francisco, created an elaborate lighting rig whose swirling colours were memorably recreated in an episode from the TV series *Mad Men*.

The opening night was a truly storied event. The *Village Voice* records the presence of Tom Wolfe, members of the Fugs and the Kennedy family, "a cavalcade of limousines" curling back round Third Avenue. Subotnick was in charge of the sound system as the night kicked off. At the time, he was in the thick of working on *Silver Apples of the Moon*, so he decided to open the evening's music with a kind of heavy pulse that would lead into the rhythmic ostinati of what would soon become the record's second side.

"So everybody was there," he recalled, "and it goes *whoom*, *whoom*, and the lights would go, and finally the strobe lights would go, and *Silver Apples of the Moon* happens, and the thing is *going off*, and everyone started *dancing* to *Silver Apples of the Moon*." He was stunned. "I could not believe it! I mean I knew it had a beat. But I'd never heard of people dancing to *that*."

For a while, in the late Sixties, The Electric Circus was the place to be. It was one of a number of nightclubs in New York City at that time that were slowly beginning to change DJ culture. The idea of a *discotheque* can be traced back to Weimar Germany. The gatherings of the Swing Jugend introduced the figure of the disc jockey who selects music based upon his own taste and expertise and not necessarily the whims of his audience. In Nazi-occupied Paris, groups of jazz-obsessed "Zazous" would gather in cafés, wearing baggy clothes and elaborate hairdos, bringing their own portable turntables. La Discothèque opened on the Rue de la Huchette in 1941, its name a portmanteau of *disque* and *bibliothèque*.

In the straitened circumstances of the Occupation, and after, in the desolation of post-war Europe, the concept of going out to dance to *records* instead of a real live band was a needs-must sort of thing. It arrived in America as high fashion. Going to a *discothèque* was, after all, *European*. At Arthur, where Terry Noel became the first DJ to mix records in a continuous flow in the mid-Sixties, the likelihood of admission was proportional to how good-looking you were. Door policy was strict. Beautiful people only.

But after its star-studded opening, The Electric Circus started to become a far more inclusive space, inspired by the psychedelic happenings on the West Coast. "I went to The Electric Circus at least once a month," DJ David Mancuso would later recall in an interview with Tim Lawrence for the latter's book about the history of disco. "Everybody was having fun, and they had good sound in there. It was very mixed, very integrated, very intense, very free, very positive."

On Valentine's Day 1970, Mancuso decided to hold a party of his own. Flyers advertised it as 'Loves Saves the Day'. The event was invite only, held in the DJ's own apartment on the corner of Broadway and Bleecker Street. No alcohol would be served, but the initials of the title indicated the kind of substitute that would be provided. Pretty soon Mancuso's parties became a regular thing. Every Saturday night, midnight till six a.m. His home was rechristened The Loft.

Around the same time, a guy called Francis Grasso started DJing at a club called The Sanctuary. He had got his start a couple of years earlier at another place, Salvation 11, when Terry Noel showed up for work three hours late, off his face on acid. Grasso, who had just come to dance, somehow got asked to take over. By 1970, he was fast becoming one of the most sought-after record spinners in the city.

Between them, Grasso and Mancuso would establish the underpinnings of a new style of music that was built up using pre-existent records. Previous DJs like Noel had pursued a kind of static continuity in variegated chunks, hailing dancers to the floor with a succession of upbeat numbers, then throwing in a ballad to make sure the punters would take regular trips to the bar. But Mancuso and Grasso wanted to structure extended narratives over the course of a long evening. Both conceived of the mix as a kind of "journey" that would take in many different types of music: classical, ethnographic recordings, pop, jazz, r&b. But crucially, DJ sets at The Loft and The Sanctuary were never fully mapped out in advance, nor entirely dictated from behind the decks. "What had emerged," argues Tim Lawrence, "was a social and egalitarian model of making music in which the DJ played in relation to the crowd, leading and following in roughly equal measure."

The DJ, Lawrence emphasises, "would improvise in order to take account of the energy and desires of the dance floor ... With improvisation came discovery (rather than familiarity), freedom (as opposed to control), and chaos (instead of order). As a result the relationship between the DJ and the crowd resembled a dynamic conversation between separate agents that, when combined, had a greater total effect than the sum of their individual parts." As Mancuso himself would emphasise in an interview from 2013, "For me The Loft is all about social progress."

It didn't take long before the atmosphere and ideals spearheaded by Grasso and Mancuso spread to other venues and other DJs. The record industry started paying attention. In 1975, the twelve-inch single was introduced. Pop songs were expanded, hyper-charged for the dancefloor with longer instrumental breaks, more space, more *rush*. The framework of extended mixes and club versions was directly derived from the practice of DJs. As records were tailored to suit the needs of the clubs, the utopian atmosphere of the disco scene spilled over into futuristic cover art and lyrics. The musical journeys of Grasso and Mancuso were transformed into trips to the stars on records like Boney M's *Nightflight to Venus* and 'Love in a UFO' by Sarah Brightman and the Aliens. When Italian producer Giorgio Moroder worked with Donna Summer on their 1977 album *I Remember Yesterday*, they self-consciously crafted every song as a progressive journey through history, ending with the visionary, electronic pulsations of 'I Feel Love'. "I wanted to conclude with a futuristic song," Moroder said, "and I decided that it had to be done with a synthesizer."

By the mid-Seventies, Morton Subotnick had come to regard *Silver Apples of the Moon* as an artistic failure. In 1971, he had recorded a piece with the Buffalo Symphony Orchestra that was "basically the first side of *Silver Apples of the Moon*," he said in an interview with Etan Rosenbloom, "with a recording going and an orchestra playing at the same time." If the piece, then, *could* be played live, Subotnick reasoned, it clearly wasn't as specific to the medium it was made for as he had hoped.

But at the same time, DJs and producers in New York lofts and nightclubs were forging a new style of music with its own unique sense of collectively-negotiated time, unthinkable without the records it was created from. What started in clubs like The Loft and The Sanctuary was then taken to a whole other level by hip hop DJs. Where Francis Grasso and David Mancuso had collaged other people's songs in the manner of Georges Braque or Kurt Schwitters sticking bus tickets and magazine clippings onto a canvas; for Grandmaster Flash, a record collection was a lump of clay or a hunk of wood to be moulded and shaped in countless different ways. Tools like the synthesizer first conceived by Subotnick at the beginning of the 1960s, along with direct descendants like the pattern sequencer and drum machine, became a crucial part of the armoury of disco producers and hip hop DJs alike. As Giorgio Moroder quickly recognised, they had become essential means for building a path to the future.

3.9 What Does Spotify Want?

When I interviewed Morton Subotnick via Skype in December 2015, we talked a lot about the way he had anticipated and contributed to the transformations music went through in the Sixties and Seventies. After we'd been talking for quite a while, I finally asked him a question that had been nagging me from almost the beginning of our conversation. In 1961, I said, you had this vision of what music might be like a hundred years in the future, but are you still thinking of what music will become a hundred years from today?

"No," he sighed. "I stopped worrying about it. But I don't think the hundred years was too far off. What I didn't anticipate was how strong popular demand is on the slowing down of certain aspects of social life. We no longer can easily distinguish entertainment from fine art. There's nothing wrong with popular art, but what's wrong with that being equivalent to fine art is that they produce it because people like it. It doesn't push the envelope – it pushes it as people like it pushed.

"I thought everything was going to happen fast," he continued, "and everybody believes it has happened fast. But the weight of popular demand slows things down from changing. That makes it very difficult for us to move.

"The best example, I suppose, is the typewriter. Originally it was getting stuck, so they built a typewriter that you couldn't write fast on so it wouldn't get stuck. And then that keyboard, that was created so you couldn't type fast, we're gonna go to Mars with! It doesn't go away! IBM tried to make one that was logical. No-one wanted to buy it. So popular demand has held back that technology. And we're ready to go to Mars – in spite of it, but with it. It's an interesting problem. So that's the way I think about the future."

I sometimes think about these words of Subotnick's in the context of collaborative filtering. That's the system that drives the recommendation algorithms on services like Amazon, Last.FM, or Spotify. The idea began with a program called RINGO created at MIT's Media Lab in 1994. "What RINGO did was simple," recalls one early user at MIT, in the book *Digital Music Wars*. "It gave you twenty-some music titles by name, then asked, one by one, whether you liked it, didn't like it, or knew it at all. That initialized the system with a small DNA of your likes and dislikes. Thereafter, when you asked for a recommendation, the program matched your DNA with that of all the others in the system. When RINGO found the best matches, it searched for music you had not heard, then recommended it. Your musical pleasure was almost certain."

Similar systems are today very widely used. Pretty much any time a website tells you it has recommendations for you, that if you like x then you've got to try y, those recommendations were probably based on some version of collaborative filtering. The platform instrumentalises the data you put into it with the promise of instant gratification. But at what cost? Almost from the very beginning of their development, some people worried that such programs might work to homogenise taste and buying patterns, rather than expand them. "The service would rarely, if ever, break out of the mould of mainstream bands," recalls one early critic of a service called Firefly, which was created by the same people behind RINGO in 1996.

Today's collaborative filtering systems are far more sophisticated than RINGO or Firefly. They rely on the collection of myriad cues given by platform users in the course of browsing, sometimes knowingly but mostly not. The processing of this information, its transformation from meaningful activities like creating playlists or sharing songs with friends, into machine-readable data, is carried out by abstruse procedures governed by software that is often proprietary in nature and opaque to its users in the manner of its operation. We feed in meaningful activity, but as Ontario University's Ganaele Langlois notes in a recent study of social media, the authority to judge how meaningful each activity is has effectively been outsourced to machines.

Few of today's online music services rely solely on collaborative filtering systems to offer up new music. They mix up the algorithmic choices with playlists generated by both ordinary users and carefully chosen experts. At least some of the people whose job it is to create Spotify playlists are brilliantly talented people with an incredibly broad taste in music and a real knack for finding songs that will appeal to different people (I know, because I'm friends with one, and he's great). But in some cases, the line between the machine-generated, user-selected, and expertly-curated is somewhat blurry. The three exist together in a self-reinforcing ecosystem. They can flow together seamlessly, like water through a tap. Ultimately, they all serve the same goal. They are not simply trying to seduce, like a mixtape from a potential date, nor just trying to make you dance, like a DJ in a club. They are after your data. Through them, your choices become information and you are formed, in turn, as a being composed of data. This is the point of social media, to generate data about its user base for sale to advertisers. And in this sense Spotify is little different from Facebook.

There is a specific temporality to social media. It is a time of perpetual manufactured crisis, in which we are constantly being prodded, reminded, and cajoled into updating, clicking our approval or disapproval, or merely checking in and registering our presence. During "real-world" crises like the earthquake in Nepal in April 2015 or the Paris terrorist attacks of later the same year, Facebook instituted a system whereby users could register that they were "safe" in order to quickly assuage the fears of their friends. In situations like that, such a system can be very useful as a source of relief for people who may not be able to get through on an overloaded phone system.

But what is interesting is the similarity in form and function between these overtly cataclysmic events and the normal running of the system on any ordinary day. "What's happening?" says Twitter when you log in. "What's on your mind?" asks Facebook. Tag people you're with. Add how you are feeling. Check in with your location. To each we are requested to respond with a litany that says "I'm here! I'm here! I'm here!" The implication is of a perpetual present. Everything is happening right now.

But if social media constructs its own time, what kind of music would be specific to that temporality? If Muzak, the radio, and records each brought about their own distinct forms, shouldn't streaming services too? What, we might ask, does Spotify want?

Technology can never fully determine its own use. Almost all systems provide for possibilities unimagined by their creators. But some uses do seem to be tacitly encouraged by systems. A particular way of working is made quite easy, while subverting that use presents challenges peculiar to the system. You can work around it, but it requires some ingenuity. Take MIDI, for instance.

The Musical Instrument Digital Interface was a protocol put together, for the most part, by Dave Smith of the synthesizer manufacturers Sequential Circuits. When it was first introduced, at the National Association of Music Merchants in January 1983, it arrived as the solution to a particularly pressing problem.

The previous quarter-century, since the release of Bob Moog and Donald Buchla's pioneering modular synthesizers, had seen the development of what keyboardist Will Gregory (of the band Goldfrapp) once described to me as an "arms race" of competing systems. With manufacturers in Europe, Asia, and America all competing to top each other's latest product, no two machines would ever synchronise with each other. The situation was becoming critical.

The record producer Martin Rushent was one of the people who was invited onto the industry discussion panel which led to the development of the MIDI standard, "because I was one of the most vigorous complainers," he said in an interview with Simon Reynolds, "saying, 'You're all bringing out all these new machines, but none of them will link together. You need to come up with some sort of standard time code they all use.'"

But MIDI did far more than simply sync up a bunch of different synths. It allowed any compatible device to act as a controller for an increasingly sophisticated range of computer software, offering an unprecedented degree of post-performance control to an instrumentalist or engineer. Notes played on a keyboard or MIDI guitar could be stretched, re-pitched, or morphed in a dizzying number of ways. Still, MIDI was ultimately a commercial product. It was limited to notions of music that were suitable to the mass market and the available means of domestic technology at the time. It was also limited by the technical limitations of its time, and the urgency of getting something out to solve what was becoming an urgent problem. As a result, a lot of the complexity and strangeness of post-war music – the extended techniques and ambiguities that Krzysztof Penderecki and others had developed, ironically, as a consequence of using electronic tools – was left, necessarily, by the wayside. For all its flexibility, at the end of the day, a MIDI note was either on or off, one or zero.

Jaron Lanier was friends with Dave Smith at the time. "When Dave made MIDI, I was thrilled," he recalls. "We felt so free – but we should have been more careful." Lanier accuses MIDI of imposing a "grid" upon the "whole of human auditory experience." Its limitations didn't matter, he claims, when Smith first knocked it together. But then it became an entrenched standard, locked-in and hard to budge. Creating a *new* MIDI would render obsolete all the old gear that had been built around it. Like Subotnick's typewriter keyboard, the weight of public approval held that back.

There are all sorts of things that you *can* do with the MIDI grid, but most people don't because, frankly, it's a pain. The system suggests certain ways of working – the use of quantised rhythms and discrete, tempered pitch classes – by making them simpler to do, making them the "default" settings. Most people tend to just go with that. Today it forms, in Lanier's words, "the lattice on which almost all the popular music you hear is built."

Spotify also encourages certain kinds of user behaviours, although it doesn't do so in nearly so explicit a fashion as MIDI. In fact, on the level of its overt actions and public statements, the company would appear to be doing everything in its power to combat them. But their sheer proliferation suggests that the very nature of the system must be providing a space in which they thrive. I might not actively want loads of bugs crawling around in my house. I might even be taking steps to get rid of the bugs whenever I see them. But you might say that if my house were still completely infested with big, fat, incredibly well-nourished creepy crawlies then maybe I had inadvertently created an environment that was conducive to the little critters, say by pouring sugar all over everything and not sweeping it up. Well, streaming platforms are a little bit like my house, and they are teeming with bugs.

Session players with names like The Hit Crew and Tribute to Macklemore record hundreds of soundalike cover versions in the hope that hapless browsers will mistake their knock-off for the real thing. The Birthday Song Crew boast a collection of 4,775 songs, from 'Happy Birthday Aariana' to 'Happy Birthday Zimena' via every conceivable name you can think of, each one identical bar the proper noun addressed in the chorus. An artist called Silhouette has several hundred instrumental tracks to their name, each one indistinguishable but for the track title. Then there are loads and loads and loads of joke ringtones, quickie dubstep versions of the latest hits, and generic new age sold one minute as yoga music and the next as a romantic soundtrack. These and other similar releases have been labelled "musical spam" by Spotify's data analysts, The Echo Nest. They tend to try and cut them out of playlists when they find them. But such songs in such quantities are the native fauna of the online music ecosphere, almost unthinkable without it.

I can't help but feel like these artists are missing a trick, though. They have, after all, gone to the trouble of actually writing and recording some music. And re-using identical tracks again and again is bound to make them relatively easy for an audio fingerprinting program to recognise and weed out. There's really no need. Since Hiller and Isaacson's *Illiac Suite*, computer-aided composition has come a long way. David Cope's program Emmy (or EMI – Experiments in Musical Intelligence) has proven itself capable of producing piano pieces in the style of Bach, Mozart, or Chopin, good enough to fool lecture theatres full of expert musicologists. And Emmy churned them out by the *thousands*. When the right kind of software is combined with the right kind of cynicism, the likes of Tribute to Macklemore can start producing an endless grey goo of new Macklemore material, even more Macklemore-ish than Macklemore himself. The original artists will no longer be able to compete with their own spambot substitutes.

Such a future for music is already hinted at in the "New-Age derivatives of some of Mozart's original compositions" that Gerd Leonhard and David Kusek promise your Taste-Mate software will soon be delivering "like water" as the long day closes. Musicians and composers are irrelevant to such a future. They appear nowhere in Leonhard and Kusek's book. We have already caught sight of the "cure" for that "cholera of the salons". Perhaps the perfect response to the standard operation of streaming media was perceived by the group Vulfpeck.

In April of 2014, the American funk band released an album called *Sleepify* onto Spotify. It consisted of ten tracks, each around thirty seconds long, and consisting of total silence. They encouraged their fans to listen to it on a loop as they slept and successfully racked up twenty thousand dollars in royalties before Spotify pulled the record from the service for unspecified terms of service violations. Maybe this is the future of music. Total silence. Forever. After all, it works. To escape it, it will be necessary to change the way we think – not just about music, but about the internet too.

Social networks and streaming media regard the net as if it were a medium that extended only through space, as if it were, essentially, just a TV you can interact with. But it's more than that. The net is not just cyberspace, it is also a kind of cyber*time*. It channels and induces its own weird sense of time passing. Robert Hassan calls it "network time." He regards the urgent sense of "real time" implied by social media to be little more than a fiction. Everything "in an instant" may be the promise held out by the salesmen of the web, but this scarcely reflects most people's daily experience of internet use, which is much more likely to be characterised by frequent delays in buffering, loading time, and the occasional crash. For Hassan, the net feels more like "connected asynchonicity" suggesting what he describes as "a smashing of the uniform and universal linearity of the clock into a billion different time contexts within the network." The disparities between those countless different "time contexts" are governed, predominantly, by differences in wealth.

For a new music to be able to address the distinctive temporality of the net and speak, once again, of the future, it will need to come to terms, not just with the specificity of the medium, but also its hold on memory, its traces, and its archives, its power to interrupt and fall out of sync. Some hint of what shape this might take is offered by Tom Lamont's story from *The Guardian* about a burnt CD in a car stereo on a long drive through California. If we want to glimpse the music of the future, it is not a question of 'Magic Carpet Ride' by Steppenwolf, but of a car full of people all singing along to the short mechanical blip on a glitched CD.

Coda: 2016

I am sitting on a train. It is a little after half past nine in the morning on the sixth of August and the sun is streaming through the tinted windows as we speed out of London. Past the Westway flyover and the stark brutalism of the Trellick Tower, the great steel gas holders of Old Oak Common cleave into the sky like landing pads for flying saucers. Acton, Ealing, Hanwell, and Southall stations fly by in a blur of yellow lines and purple signage. Then on through ever greener pastures, the suburban semis and sprawling carparks of Hayes & Harlington, the retail parks and Tesla car showrooms of West Drayton, soon giving way to golf courses, treatment works, and open fields.

I'm on my way to a music festival near Reading, called Supernormal. Later today I will see a harpist called Áine O'Dwyer plucking at strings with her feet whilst lying on the floor beneath a green baize cloth. I will attend a workshop, delivered by the artist group AAS, about an imaginary discipline called Holectics, "the precise purpose and function of which is in a state of constant, molecular, flux." I will take part in an improvised noise choir in which melodies and drones will be spontaneously drawn from a few dozen participants using no more than randomly selected vowels and consonants for guidance.

Almost as interesting as the programmed performances themselves will be the venue hosting them. A listed gothic pile and childhood home to James Bond creator Ian Fleming, since the 1950s Braziers Park has operated as "a continuing experiment in the advantages and problems of living in a group." According to its website, Braziers Park is "one of the oldest secular communities in the UK." In her autobiography, Marianne Faithfull, who grew up there, recalls seeing communards "fucking like rabbits...everywhere" and the enacting of "quasi-mystical rituals." People still live there communally to this day and the house hosts several artist-in-residence programmes. Supernormal Festival has been held there, once a year, since 2010. Áine O'Dwyer's dada harpistry will take place in the house's wood-panelled Victorian drawing room, surrounded by china plates and colonial busts.

My part in the proceedings will be to chair a panel discussion about artistic collaboration. Sam Cook and Sam Underwood are two musicians brought together on the Brazier's Park artist-in-residency programme earlier in the year, who will be spending the weekend marching about the site, performing on instruments of their own devising, made from found materials. During our talk, they will recall "a really good moment on the residency when we were all brought together, not only into the community of Brazier's Park, but also encouraged to form our *own* community. We talked about a collective consciousness. I think for us, it was important to just start making sound, because it brought us together without having to discuss what we were doing."

But when I go on to say that perhaps the forms of collaboration that arise spontaneously amongst improvising musicians could provide a model for other forms of community – even political associations – another artist and writer, Claire Potter, will express a certain hesitation. "That's *problematic*," she will say.

"I think it's very dangerous," Sam Belinfante, also on the panel, will agree, "to buy into this idea of music being this universal emancipatory thing for good, where actually it can lead you astray – like the sirens on the rocks."

It's a worry. By the 1930s, Fourier's dream of a city ruled by music had devolved into Nazi party officials filling up the parterre at Bayreuth. The Italian Futurists had shifted from the desecration of all myths, to the building of new myths in celebration of Mussolini. Walter Benjamin calls this the "aestheticisation of politics" – a sure pathway to fascism. But if the music of the future is forced to abandon totality, to eschew narrative for small acts, carefully finessed, won't someone else step in to write the next chapter of the story for us? I think there is a degree to which the rejection of "the aestheticisation of the political" as necessarily fascist is another version of the rejection of utopia, and of the lumping together of communism and fascism with all philosophical programmes for social transformation that is an essential part of the neoliberal project that began at Mont Pelerin in 1947. We still need some equivalent of Ray Bradbury's Time Traveller to fabricate a future capable of navigating this terrain. Acts of hubris, doomed to failure, may be required more urgently today than ever before.

These thoughts will trouble me, shuttling between the foreground and background of my mind for much of the rest of the day as I wander the festival later that evening, watching bands, catching up with friends. But for now, all this stays in the future.

Still sitting on the train, from the window I can see the idling forklifts of construction firms on the edge of Slough. The train wheels no longer clatter rhythmically against the tracks as they did in Wagner's day. There is just a steady low-end hum, like an electric hand-drier. On top of that, I can hear the repetitive sibilance of hi-hats leaking from a nearby passenger's earbuds. The occasional *swoosh* of inter-carriage doors opening and closing. A harmonic *bong* introduces on-board announcements, "The next station is... Reading." Somebody's phone goes off and the ring tone tinnily synthesises the opening bars of Franz Liszt's *Liebestraum*.

It is not quite the "great symphony of electricity" conjured by Albert Robida. In his *The Twentieth Century*, he had described the sounds on the streets of his future Paris. "Thousands of musical chimes and bell sounds coming from the sky," he wrote in 1882, "from homes, and even from the ground, merge into one vibrant, merry, metallic melody that Beethoven, could he have heard it, would have named the great symphony of electricity." Today's streets – and today's train carriages – do not quite sound like that. They are just as awash with electrical sounds. But their combination would be as incomprehensible to Beethoven as most modern music.

I slip on a pair of headphones and turn on the first piano sonata by Elliott Carter. Hesitant at first, soon the notes start to tumble from the speakers in fitful exuberance. First performed in 1946, it is a strange and sinuous piece of music, marked by dramatic changes of tempo and metre that somehow never feel abrupt or forced. For Carter, the piece marked the tentative beginnings of a new approach to music. At the time of its composition, Carter wrote to Edgard Varèse explaining that the piano sonata represented his newfound interest in "the plastic flow of music and in contrasting rates of change ... My music," he explained at the end of the letter, "is essentially a kinetic projection of ideas, using perspectives of time."

The technique he employs in this work, later dubbed "temporal modulation" to indicate the way the overall structure is determined by changes in time rather than harmonic colour, would find an even clearer exposition in his string quartet of five years later. Much of the tension in this later work derives from the feeling that the different voices are sometimes slipping away from each other or rushing to catch up, such that at times all four string instruments are effectively operating in entirely separate time zones, one surging forward towards the change of metre that's just about to happen, another still dragging its feet in the tempo of a few bars back, and so on. He speaks of the different temporal strands of his works as distinct "characters." His music from this period possesses a narrative quality closer to that of cinema, with its montage of interlocking storylines, than to traditional music. In interviews, Carter is as likely to cite the influence of Sergei Eisenstein or Jean Cocteau as any contemporary composer.

But what strikes me most as I listen to Carter's piano sonata now is this tumbling sensation to the notes – particularly in some of the faster, more rhythmically complex passages. It reminds me of feeling that same tumbling sensation listening to the beats that Jlin was playing at the Borealis Festival, in Bergen back in March 2016. The music Jlin played that night had seemed to wrap around you, to drift and surge and pull you forwards with it. It played with time as if it were something plastic in a way very similar to Elliott Carter's music from the mid-twentieth century. Each are possessed of a flow that feels mysteriously unquantifiable and indivisible.

It starts me thinking about Robert Hassan's idea of "network time" as "a smashing of the uniform and universal linearity of the clock into a billion different time contexts within the network." In a strange way, Carter's music seems to anticipate the "connected asynchronicity" of Hassan's networks, notes pressing forward in dynamic disequilibrium, each instrumental "character" occupying its own distinct time context. Carter's many-stranded musical narratives point forwards from cinema's montage of attractions towards a temporal montage. Slowly shifting plate tectonics erupt, here and there, into explosive sonic volcanos where the different instrumental lines collide and break apart again. A sudden chord can seem like an earthquake on the International Date Line, tearing time apart at the seams.

Drifting into a sort of reverie, half-hypnotised by the speeding power lines visible through the train window, I start thumbing the screen of my phone, without thinking. Exiting the device's music app, Carter's piano sonata still playing, I log in to Twitter. Someone retweets a flyer for a club the previous night in Sheffield called 'Visions of the Future'. It is bedecked with retro Gernsbackian spacemen and Martian landscapes, straight off the cover of *Fantastic Stories*. Fancy dress is encouraged. In another tweet, an online music magazine is promising an in-depth analysis of every track played in the background of a recent livestream by the r&b singer Frank Ocean. Another article talks about a band who wrote their album over Facebook's instant messenger service. Brian Eno's official Twitter account, @dark_shark, posts an image of Sun Ra's old business card. "Why buy old sounds?" it asks, "Buy new sounds from the future!" A composer called Andy Ingamells posts a photo from the Darmstadt summer school for new music, in which someone is sitting on the floor, apparently vacuum-cleaning an accordion. An automated account called Graphic Score Bot posts two new randomly generated scores: a five-line stave headed by a bass clef bearing four large circles of different colours and sizes, sometimes overlapping three or four different lines; and then a single sentence, "You can only make one dot at a time." Another tweet is plugging a forthcoming opera performance. It is to be transmitted live as a fully holographic show from a hi-tech studio miles away to a warehouse in Topeka. They're playing *Don Giovanni*. The author Hari Kunzru asks, "Writers, do you also see fake profiles tweeting out slightly random 'quotes' from your internet-accessible work?" William Gibson, who coined the word "cyberspace" in his fiction from the early 1980s, replies simply "yep." And as if on cue, another account I follow tweets Gibson's famous line that "The future is already here, it's just unevenly distributed." Only they word it slightly differently, and attribute it to somebody else.

Twitter presents itself as a flowing stream in real-time. But in fact it's a far weirder mesh of many different times in uneasy counterpoint. People around the world in different time zones, hooked up via different connection speeds, some with super-fast broadband, others on a sluggish dial-up connection, or waggling their device in the air searching for 3G. There are posts generated automatically by bots, or scheduled in advance by client software, referring to things that will happen in the future, or commenting on events happening now, replying to other posts from days or weeks ago. But the whole thing is able to co-exist on a single scroll bar, unfurling like train tracks over a horizon.

Bong, "We are now arriving –" and suddenly I'm jolted out of my social-media haze. Hurriedly I start gathering up my things "– at Reading." What had felt like a few seconds must have been more like twenty minutes. The time just seemed to get swallowed up. Any thought of the work I'd intended to get done on this journey now out of the window, I rush down the aisle to the exit.

Brushing past seats too tightly-packed, an aphorism springs to mind from a recent book called *The Age of Earthquakes*, co-authored by Douglas Coupland, Shumon Basar, and the curator Hans Ulrich Obrist. "But the more you offload your memories onto hard drives and into the Cloud, the more your memory becomes, in a very real sense, artificial. Technically, someone who spends all day in front of a screen has no memories of their own except for going to the fridge for a Coke..."

These days, my music collection – like the Elliott Carter track I had on until just a moment ago – is stored, alongside all my other documents and photos, on a Cloud storage site. For a small monthly fee, I have a virtually limitless space to keep stuff in, and access it whenever I need it. But somehow it doesn't quite feel mine in the way it did when it was stored on discs of black vinyl or shimmering plastic on a shelf in my room. Everything is there, nothing need be thrown away, but lacking a sense of dimension, it seems also to lack any sense of *protension*. "Imagine hypothetically that I have an infinite memory," Bernard Stiegler writes in the third book of his *Technics and Time*. "I thus remember every second and fraction of a second exactly identically... There is no longer any difference, because there has been no selection: time has not *passed*. Nothing has happened nor can happen to me... no passage of time is possible. Time has ceased to exist."

This is the condition of the online world, in which every trace is meticulously preserved, but web pages start to mysteriously disappear after an average of one hundred days. They may get deliberately scrubbed, they may die with the company that hosted them, or they may just fade away from neglect. Link rot is pervasive, but it's also capricious in a way markedly different to the unreliability of memory.

Web archivists like the Internet Archive are trying, valiantly, to preserve the disappearing web. It's an incredibly valuable resource, staffed by heroic individuals. But the sheer volume of stuff they scoop up precludes meaningful classification. "You can't search it the way you can search the Web," noted a 2015 *New Yorker* profile, "because it's too big and what's in there isn't sorted, or indexed, or catalogued in any of the many ways in which a paper archive is organized; it's not ordered in any way at all, except by URL and by date." History, as a story that means something, is replaced by the blunt accumulation of data points, like mp3s on a Napster user's hard drive. Time becomes directionless, incapable of formulating its next chapter. The machines grinds on but the world stops.

Now I'm in the vestibule between coaches. The train pulls into the station. I press the button to open the doors, and step out onto the platform.

Bibliography

Attali, J. *Noise: The Political Economy of Music*, Massumi, B. (trans.), University of Minnesota Press, 1985

Bakhtin, M. *Rabelais and His World*, Iswolsky, H. (trans.), Indiana University Press, 1984

Bataille, G. *The Absence of Myth: Writings on Surrealism*, Richardson, M. (trans.), Verso, 2006

Barrett, G.D. 'Between Noise and Language: The Sound Installations and Music of Peter Ablinger' in *Mosaic*, Vol.42, No.4, 2009

Beaurain, N. 'Fourier: Où la science-fiction se fait opera quand le travail devient plaisir' in *Actualité de Fourier,* Lefebvre, H. (ed.), Éditions Anthropos, 1975

Beckett, L. 'Wagner and His Critics', *The Wagner Companion*, Burbidge, P. & Sutton, R. (eds), Faber, 1979

Beecher, J. *Charles Fourier: The Visionary and His World*, University of California Press, 1992

Bellamy, E. *Looking Backward*, Applewood, 2000

Berger, K. *Bach's Cycle, Mozart's Arrow*, University of California Press, 2007

Berlioz, H. *A Treatise on Modern Instrumentation and Orchestration*, Clarke, M.C. (trans.), Novello, Ewer & Co., 1882;

—. *Evenings in the Orchestra*, Barzun, J. (trans.), University of Chicago Press, 1999

Bernstein, D. *The San Francisco Tape Music Center 1960s: Counterculture and the Avantgarde*, University of California Press, 2008

Bohn, J. M. *The Music of American Composer Lejaren Hiller and an Examination of His Early Works Involving Technology*, Mellen, 2004

Boime, A. *Art in an Age of Civil Struggle, 1848–1871*, University of Chicago Press, 2007

Borges, J.L. *Fictions*, Hurley, A. (trans.), Penguin, 2000

Bull, M. *Sound Moves: iPod Culture and Urban Experience*, Routledge, 2007

Burkart, P. & McCourt, T. *Digital Music Wars: Ownership and Control of the Celestial Jukebox*, Rowman & Littlefield, 2006

Busoni, F. *Sketch of a New Aesthetic of Music*, Baker, T. (trans.), Schirmer, 1911

Cage, J. *Silence*, Wesleyan University Press, 1973

—. *Empty Words: Writings '73–'78*, Wesleyan University Press, 1981

Chun, W.H.K. *Updating to Remain the Same: Habitual New Media*, MIT Press, 2016

Clarke, I.F. *The Pattern of Expectation*, Jonathan Cape, 1979

Collins, G.R. & Collins, C.C. *Camillo Sitte: The Birth of Modern City Planning*, Dover, 1986

Cope, D. *Virtual Music: Computer Synthesis of Musical Style*, MIT Press, 2001

Crittenden, C. *Johann Strauss and Vienna: Operetta and the Politics of Popular Culture*, Cambridge University Press, 2000

Deaville, J. 'Franz Brendel's Reconciliation Address' in *Richard Wagner and His World*, Grey, T.S. (ed.), Princeton University Press, 2009

Delany, S.R. *Longer Views*, Wesleyan University Press, 1996

Deschamps, E. 'Les Appartements à Louer' in *Paris, ou Le Livre des Cent-et-Un*, Tome Huitième, Schmerber, 1832

Desroche, H. 'Images and Echoes of Owenism in Nineteenth-Century France' in *Robert Owen: Prophet of the Poor*, Pollard, S. & Salt, J. (eds), 1971

Doctorow, C. 'Foreword' in *Sound Unbound*, Miller, P.D. (ed.), MIT Press, 2008

Duveyrier, C. 'La Ville Nouvelle ou Le Paris des Saint-Simoniens' in *Paris, ou Le Livre des Cent-et-Un*, Tome Huitième, Schmerber, 1832

Edwards, P.N. *The Closed World: Computers and the Politics of Discourse in Cold War America*, MIT Press, 1997

Faris, A. *Jacques Offenbach*, Faber & Faber, 1980

Fauquet, J.–M. 'The *Grand Traité d'instrumentation*' in *The Cambridge Companion to Berlioz*, Bloom, P. (ed.), Cambridge University Press, 2000

—. 'Euphonia and the Utopia of the Orchestra as Society' in *Berlioz: Scenes from the life and work*, Bloom, P. (ed.), Rochester, New York: Rochester Press, 2008

Fikentscher, K. *You Better Work! Underground Dance Music in New York*, Wesleyan, 2000

Fischer, W.B. *The Empire Strikes Out: Kurd Lasswitz, Hans Dominik, and the Development of German Science Fiction*, Bowling Green State University Popular Press, 1984

Foreman, R. *The Manifestos and Essays*, Theatre Communications Group, 2013

Fourier, C. 'Théorie de l'unité universelle' *Oeuvres complètes*, Vol.4, Société pour la Propagation et pour la Réalisation de la Théorie de Fourier, 1841

—. *The Utopian Vision of Charles Fourier: Selected Texts on Work, Love, and Passionate Attraction*, Beecher, J. & Bienvenu, R. (trans. & ed.), Jonathan Cape, 1972

Franklin, A. 'The Ruins of Paris in 4875' in *Investigations of the Future*, Stableford, B. (ed. and trans.), Black Coat Press, 2012

Gann, K. *No Such Thing As Silence: John Cage's 4'33''*, Yale University Press, 2010

Gautier, T. 'Future Paris' in *Investigations of the Future*, Stableford, B. (ed. and trans.), Black Coat, 2012

Glinsky, A. *Theremin: Ether Music & Espionage*, University of Illinois Press, 2005

Goldstein, P. *Copyright's Highway: From Gutenberg to the Celestial Jukebox*, Revised Edition, Stanford University Press, 2003

Gould, S.J. *Time's Arrow, Time's Cycle*, Penguin, 1987

Grandville, J.J. *Un autre monde*, Fournier, 1844

Greenberg, C. 'Modernist Painting' in *Modern Art and Modernism: A Critical Anthology*, Frascina, F. & Harrison, C. (eds), Harper & Row, 1982

Griffiths, J. *Pip Pip: A Sideways Look at Time*, Flamingo, 1999

Hanslick, E. *Vom Musikalisch-Schönen: Ein Beitrag zur Revision der Aesthetik der Tonkunst*, Weigel, 1922

Harvey, D. *A Brief History of Neoliberalism*, Oxford University Press, 2007

Hiller, L. & Isaacson, L. *Experimental Music*, Greenwood, 1979

Hodgkinson, T. *Music and the Myth of Wholeness*, MIT Press, 2016

Hueffer, F. *Richard Wagner and the Music of the Future*, Cambridge University Press, 2009

Jarvis, R. *The Romantic Period: The Intellectual and Cultural Context of English Literature, 1789–1830*, Pearson, 2004

de Jouvenel, B. *The Ethics of Redistribution*, Cambridge
  University Press, 1951
—. *The Art of Conjecture*, Lary, N. (trans.), Weidenfeld &
  Nicolson, 1967
Just, T. 'After Opera' in *Arcana VII: Musicians on Music*, Zorn,
  J. (ed.), Hips Road/Tzadik, 2014
Kahn, D. *Noise, Water, Meat: A History of Sound in the Arts*,
  MIT Press, 2001
Karnes, K.C. *Music, Criticism, and the Challenge of History:
  Shaping Modern Musical Thought in Late Nineteenth-Century
  Vienna*, Oxford University Press, 2008
—. *A Kingdom Not of This World: Wagner, the Arts, and
  Utopian Visions in Fin-de-Siècle Vienna*, Oxford
  University Press, 2013
Kassabian, A. *Ubiquitous Listening: Affect, Attention, and
  Distributed Subjectivity*, University of California Press, 2013
Kerman, J. *Opera as Drama*, Knopf, 1956
Kern Holoman, D. *Berlioz*, Faber, 1999
Koley, S. 'Ordoliberalism and the Austrian School' in *The
  Oxford Handbook of Austrian Economics*, Boettke, P.J. &
  Coyne, C.J. (eds), Oxford University Press, 2015
Koselleck, R. *Futures Past: On the Semantics of Historical Time*,
  Tribe, K. (trans.), Columbia University Press, 2004
Kramer, J.D. *The Time of Music*, Schirmer, 1988
Kramer, L. *Opera and Modern Culture*, University of
  California Press, 2007
Kusek, D. & Leonhard, G. *The Future of Music: Manifesto
  for the Digital Music Revolution*, Berklee, 2005
Lacoue-Labarthe, P. *Musica Ficta*, McCarren, F. (trans.),
  Stanford University Press, 1994
Langlois, G. *Meaning in the Age of Social Media*, Palgrave
  Macmillan, 2014
Lanier, *You Are Not a Gadget*, Penguin, 2011
Lanza, J. *Elevator Music: A Surreal History of Muzak, Easy
  Listening, and Other Moodsong*, University of Michigan
  Press, 2004
Lasswitz, K. *Two Planets*, Rudnick, H.H. (trans.), Popular
  Library, 1971

—. 'To The Absolute Zero of Existence: A Story From 2371' in *The Black Mirror and Other Stories*, Rottensteiner, F. (ed.), Mitchell, M. (trans.), Wesleyan University Press, 2008

Lawrence, T. *Love Saves the Day: A History of American Dance Culture, 1970–1979*, Duke University Press, 2003

Leube, K. 'Efforts that Failed: On Friedrich A. von Hayek in War and Peace' in *An Austrian in Italy: Festschrift in Honour of Professor Dario Antiseri*, De Mucci, R. & Leube, K. (eds), Rubnettino, 2012

Locke, R.P. *Music, Musicians and the Saint-Simonians*, University of Chicago Press, 1986

Lukács, G. *The Historical Novel*, Mitchell, H. & Mitchell, S. (trans.), Merlin, 1962

McDonald, M. *Varèse: Astronomer in Sound*, Kahn & Averill, 2003

McLuhan, M. *Understanding Media*, Sphere, 1967

Maconie, R. *Other Planets: The Music of Karlheinz Stockhausen*, Scarecrow, 2005

Mahoney, D.J. *Bertrand de Jouvenel: The Conservative Liberal and the Illusions of Modernity*, ISI, 2005

Mann, T. 'Coming to Terms with Richard Wagner' in *German Essays on Music*, Hermand, J. & Gilbert, M. (eds), Continuum, 1994

Marinetti, F.T. *Critical Writings*, Berghaus, G. (ed.), Thompson, D. (trans.), Farrar, Strauss & Giroux, 2006

Mercier, L.-S. *Memoirs of the Year Two Thousand Five Hundred*, Hooper, W. (trans.), Dobson, 1795

Miller, H. *The Air-Conditioned Nightmare*, New Directions, 1970

Mirowski, P. *The Road from Mont Pelerin: The Making of the Neoliberal Thought Collective*, Harvard University Press, 2015

Newark, C. 'Metaphors for Meyerbeer' in *Journal of the Royal Musical Association*, Vol.127, No.1, 2002

Newman, E. *The Life of Richard Wagner: Volume 2, 1848–1860*, Cambridge University Press, 1976

—. *The Life of Richard Wagner, Volume 4: 1866–1883*, Cassell, 1947

Panchasi, R. *Future Tense: The Culture of Anticipation in France between the Wars*, Cornell University Press, 2009

Pateman, R. *Chaos and Dancing Star: Wagner's Politics, Wagner's Legacy*, University Press of America, 2002

Pincus-Witten, R. *Postminimalism into Maximalism: American Art, 1966–1986*, UMI, 1987

Praeger, F. *Wagner As I Knew Him*, Longmans, Green, & Co., 1892

Pratella, B. 'Manifesto of Futurist Musicians' in *Futurist Manifestos*, Apollonio, U. (ed.), MFA, 2001

Rehding, A. 'Inventing Liszt's life: early biography and autobiography' in *The Cambridge Companion to Liszt*, Hamilton, K. (ed.), Cambridge University Press, 2005

Reynolds, S. *Totally Wired: Postpunk Interviews and Overviews*, Faber, 2009

—. *Retromania: Pop Culture's Addiction to Its Own Past*, Faber, 2011

—. 'Maximal Nation' in *Pitchfork*, http://pitchfork.com/features/articles/8721-maximal-nation/, 2011

Rivers, C. *Maximalism: The Graphic Design of Decadence and Excess*, Rotovision, 2008

Robida, A. *The Twentieth Century*, Willems, P. (trans.), Wesleyan University Press, 2004

Russell, D. *Popular Music in England, 1840–1914: A Social History*, Manchester University Press, 1987

Russolo, L. *The Art of Noises*, Filiou, R. (trans.), Something Else, 1967

Saint-Simon, C.H. & Thierry, A. *De la réorganisation de la société Européenne*, Chez Adrien Égron, 1814

Saint-Simon, C.H. *New Christianity*, Smith, J.E. (trans.), Cousins, 1834

Scherer, F.M. *Quarter Notes and Bank Notes: The Economics of Music Composition in the Eighteenth and Nineteenth Centuries*, Princeton University Press, 2004

Schreffler, A.C. 'Varèse and the Technological Sublime; or, How Ionisation Went Nuclear' in *Edgard Varése: Composer, Sound Sculptor, Visionary*, Meyer, F. & Zimmerman, H. (eds), Boydell Press, 2006

Schumann, R. *The Letters of Robert Schumann*, Storck, K. (ed.), Bryant, H. (trans.), Arno Press, 1979

Scott, D. B. *Sounds of the Metropolis*, New York: Oxford University Press, 2008 de Selincourt, B. 'Music and Duration' in *Reflections on Art*, Langer, S.K. (ed.), Johns Hopkins, 1958

Sessa, A.D. *Richard Wagner and the English*, Farleigh Dickinson, 1979

Shannon, C.E. 'Information Theory' in *Miscellaneous Writings*, Sloane, N.J.A. & Wyner, A.D. (eds), Bell Labs, 1994

Shapiro, P. *Turn the Beat Around*, Faber, 2005

Spotts, F. *Bayreuth: A History of the Wagner Festival*, Yale University Press, 1994

Steinmetz, R. *György Ligeti: Music of the Imagination*, Faber, 2003

Sterne, J. 'Sounds Like the Mall of America: Programmed Music and the Architectonics of Commercial Space' in *Ethnomusicology*, Vol.41, No.1, 1997

—. 'The mp3 as cultural artifact', *New Media & Society*, Vol.8, No.5, 2006

—. *MP3: The Meaning of a Format*, Duke University Press, 2012

Stevenson, R. *Modernist Fiction: An Introduction*, University of Kentucky Press, 1992

Bernard Stiegler, *Technics and Time, 3: Cinematic Time and the Question of Malaise*, Stephen Barker (trans.), Stanford, California: Stanford University Press, 2011

Szwed, J. *Space is the Place: The Life and Times of Sun Ra*, Canongate, 2000

Tannenbaum, M. *Conversations with Stockhausen*, Butchart, D. (trans.), Oxford University Press, 1987

Taruskin, R. *Music in the Early Twentieth Century*, Oxford University Press, 2010

Taylor, R. *Franz Liszt: The Man and the Musician*, Grafton, 1986

Tenney, J. *Meta Hodos and Meta Meta Hodos*, Second Edition, Frog Peak, 1988

Thompson, E.P. 'Time, Work-Discipline, and Industrial Capitalism' in *Past & Present*, No.38, 1967

Toop, D. *Ocean of Sound*, Serpent's Tail, 2001

Tresch, J. *The Romantic Machine: Utopian Science and Technology after Napoleon*, University of Chicago Press, 2012

Varèse, E. 'The Liberation of Sound' in *Audio Culture: Readings in Modern Music*, Cox, C. & Warner, D. (eds), Continuum, 2006

Varèse, L. *Varèse: A Looking-Glass Diary*, Norton, 1972

Vergo, P. *Art in Vienna, 1898–1918*, Phaidon, 1981

Verne, J. *Paris in the Twentieth Century*, Howard, R. (trans.), Ballantine, 1997

Wagner, R. 'Appendix to Judaism in Music' in *Richard Wagner's Prose Works, Volume III*, Ellis, W.A. (trans.), Reeves, 1892

—. 'Zukunftsmusik' in *Richard Wagner's Prose Works, Volume III*, Ellis, W.A. (trans.), Reeves, 1892

—. *My Life*, Whittall, M. (ed.), Gray, A. (trans.), Cambridge University Press, 1983

—. *The Artwork of the Future*, Ellis, W.A. (trans.), Dodo, 2008

Walker, A. *Franz Liszt: The Weimar Years, 1848-1861*, Cornell University Press, 1993

Walshe, J. '(Some Other) Notes on Conceptualisms' in *MusikTexte*, No.145, 2015

Weber, W. *The Great Transformation of Musical Taste: Concert Programming from Haydn to Brahms*, Cambridge University Press, 2008

Weidenaar, R. *Magic Music from the Telharmonium*, Scarecrow Press, 1995

Wirth, M. *A Window to the World: The European Forum Alpbach 1945 to 2015*, European Forum Alpbach, 2015

Zhdanov, A. *On Literature, Music and Philosophy*, Lawrence & Wishart, 1950

Acknowledgments

First of all, I would like to thank Tariq Goddard for asking me to write this book in the first place – and, perhaps even more, for his patience and forbearance while I slowly scraped it together. I would also like to thank all the friends who read and commented on early drafts, especially Houman Barekat, Oliver Dutton, Owen Hatherley, Agata Pyzik, and Gwenno Saunders. Thanks to Davorka Begović for inviting me to talk at Izlog Suvremenog Zvuka in Zagreb, to Peter Meanwell for inviting me to Borealis Festival, Sofie Ringstad for inviting me to Ultima Festival, to Matilda Strang for inviting me to Supernormal Festival, to Olatz de Solaeche for inviting me to Eurockéenes Festival, and to Patricia Hofmann, Michaela Mainberger, and Berno Odo Polzer for inviting me to MaerzMusik in Berlin. Thanks also to Luke Turner and John Doran at *The Quietus*, Derek Walmsley, Frances Morgan, Chris Bohn, and Emily Bick at *The Wire*, Josh Baines at *Thump*, and all at *Fact*, *Frieze*, *RBMA Daily*, *Art Review*, and *Exeunt* for commissioning me to write pieces that introduced me to many of the interview subjects and led me down many of the thought paths that would end up in this book. Most of all thanks to my wife, Thanh Mai, for her love and support and encouragement; without whom this book would probably never have got finished.

Repeater Books

is dedicated to the creation of a new reality. The landscape of twenty-first-century arts and letters is faded and inert, riven by fashionable cynicism, egotistical self-reference and a nostalgia for the recent past. Repeater intends to add its voice to those movements that wish to enter history and assert control over its currents, gathering together scattered and isolated voices with those who have already called for an escape from Capitalist Realism. Our desire is to publish in every sphere and genre, combining vigorous dissent and a pragmatic willingness to succeed where messianic abstraction and quiescent co-option have stalled: abstention is not an option: we are alive and we don't agree.